CHICKENS, DUCKS AND BEES

VISIT OUR HOW TO WEBSITE AT WWW.HOWTO.CO.UK

At www.howto.co.uk you can engage in conversation with our authors – all of whom have 'been there and done that' in their specialist fields. You can get access to special offers and additional content but most importantly you will be able to engage with, and become a part of, a wide and growing community of people just like yourself.

At www.howto.co.uk you'll be able to talk and share tips with people who have similar interests and are facing similar challenges in their lives. People who, just like you, have the desire to change their lives for the better – be it through moving to a new country, starting a new business, growing their own vegetables, or writing a novel.

At www.howto.co.uk you'll find the support and encouragement you need to help make your aspirations a reality.

How To Books strive to present authentic, inspiring, practical information in their books. Now, when you buy a title from How To Books, you get even more than just words on a page.

CHICKENS, DUCKS AND BEES

A BEGINNER'S GUIDE TO KEEPING LIVESTOCK IN THE GARDEN

Paul Peacock

SPRING HILL

Published by How To Books Ltd
Spring Hill House, Spring Hill Road
Begbroke, Oxford OX5 1RX
Tel: (01865) 375794. Fax: (01865) 379162
info@howtobooks.co.uk
www.howtobooks.co.uk

How To Books greatly reduce the carbon footprint of their books by sourcing
their typesetting and printing in the UK.

British Library Cataloguing in Publication Data
A catalogue record for this book is available from the British Library

ISBN 978 1 905862 57 3

Text illustrations by Rebecca Peacock
Produced for How To Books by Deer Park Productions, Tavistock
Typeset by PDQ Typesetting, Newcastle-under-Lyme, Staffs.
Printed and bound in Great Britain by Bell & Bain Ltd, Glasgow

NOTE: The material contained in this book is set out in good faith for general
guidance and no liability can be accepted for loss or expense incurred as a result
of relying in particular circumstances or statements made in the book. The laws
and regulations are complex and liable to change, and readers should check the
current position with the relevant authorities before making personal
arrangements.

CONTENTS

Chapter 1: Introduction to Chickens, Ducks and Bees   **1**
Keeping animals for food   1
Why times are changing   3
Why chickens, ducks and bees?   3
Keeping animals won't save you money   3
Three great reasons for keeping animals   4
Teacup philosophy   4
Becoming more self-sufficient   5

Chapter 2: Organising the Garden for Livestock   **7**
Finding out all you can before buying your livestock   7
Hens   8
Ducks   9
Bees   10

PART ONE: CHICKENS   **11**

Chapter 3: Introduction to Chickens   **13**
The hen and what she needs   13
Having time to look after your hens   14
Eating the meat   15
Using the feathers   15
Enjoying fun and companionship   16
Clearing up poo   16
Enjoying new-laid eggs   16
What do your chickens need?   17
Do you need a cockerel?   18
Where to put your hens   18
Housing your hens   19
Siting the hut   20
Spare housing   20
Stopping your hens fighting   20
Temperature   21
Clipping wings   21

A word about sickness 22
What do hens really enjoy? 23
Checking that you have permission to keep hens 23
Dispatching your hens 25
Getting advice 26

Chapter 4: Handling Your Hens **27**
Why would you want to hold your hens? 27
How to hold a hen 30
Releasing your hen 30
Using a carry box 31

Chapter 5: How To Feed Your Hens **32**
The importance of protein 33
The best ways of delivering food 34
Feeding hens in the city 34
Pellets or mash 35
Using a gravity feeder 35
Providing water for your hens 36
Providing calcium in your hens' diet 37
How much do chickens eat? 37
Providing the 'extras' 38

Chapter 6: Housing Hens **40**
Providing ventilation 42
Materials 42
Nesting boxes 43
Providing perches 44
Providing a litter tray 45
Providing a big enough run 46
Siting the hut 47
Moving the position of the hut and run 47
Storing food 48
Using a broody box 48
Building your own chicken hut 49
Introducing hens to their new home 51
Inroducing hens to each other 52

Chapter 7: How To Keep Your Hens Healthy and Clean   **53**
Cleaning the hutch   53
Don't over-disinfect   54
Cleaning the nest boxes   55
Cleaning feeders   55

Chapter 8: Choosing your Birds   **56**
What are the advantages of keeping a cockerel?   56
How to buy hens   57
Breeds suitable for everyone   59

Chapter 9: How To Recognise When Things Are Going Wrong   **65**
Apple cider vinegar (ACV)   65
Other additives   66
Hens sitting in the corner, hardly feeding or drinking   66
Hens with feathers missing   67
White encrusting at the base of the feathers   67
Birds with scaly legs   67
Lots of diarrhoea and hungry birds   68
Pale combs and reduced egg production   68
Wheezing birds   68

Chapter 10: What Makes a Chicken Tick?   **69**
The chicken gut and how it works   69
How hens make eggs   70
The moult   71
Broodiness   71
Crumbs   72
What are you going to do about cockerels?   73
Caring for your hens around the year   73

PART TWO: DUCKS   **77**

Chapter 11: Introduction to Ducks   **79**
Good gardeners   79
What you need to keep ducks   80
Housing your ducks   80

Feeding your ducks 81
Using your ducks for meat and eggs 82
Handling ducks 83
Duck life 83

Chapter 12: Feeding Your Ducks **84**
Organising your ducks' diet 84
Finisher pellets 85
Providing water 85
Allowing your ducks to forage 86
Offering oyster shell 86
Making grit available 87
Providing extras 87

Chapter 13: Housing Ducks **88**
Making the housing strong 88
Waterproofing the duck house 89
Siting the duck house 89
Lifting the hut 89
Roosting 90
Nesting 90
Fumigating 91
The run 91

Chapter 14: Keeping Ducks for Eggs **92**
Choosing ducks for egg production 92
What's the egg like? 94
Where your ducks lay 94
Storing duck eggs 95
The good duck egg guide 95
Cooking with duck eggs 95
How do ducks lay eggs? 96

Chapter 15: Duck Breeds **97**
How to buy ducks 97
Buying in trios 98
Choosing your ducks 98

Keeping bantams   102

Chapter 16: Duck Diseases   **104**
Tips for healthy ducks   104

PART THREE: BEES   **109**
Chapter 17: Beekeeping   **111**

Chapter 18: Bee Anatomy   **114**
The respiratory and circulatory system   114
The exoskeleton   116
Wings and legs   116
The head   117
Inside the bee   118
The sting   118
Differences between the castes   118

Chapter 19: Getting Started   **120**
Asking for advice from experienced beekeepers   120
Wearing protective clothing   121
Using a smoker   122
Buying a hive tool   123
Using buckets   124
Blowtorch   125
Feeders   125
Varroa control requirements   127
Choosing the hive   127
The brood box   128
Rearranging the furniture   129
The supers   129
The lid   130
The stand   130
A mentor   130
Races of bees   131
Castes of bee   131
How to buy bees   134

Chapter 20: The Beekeeping Year **136**
Warm way/cold way 138
The development of bees 139
Orientation flights 140

Chapter 21: Beekeeping Techniques **141**
What are you looking for in the hive? 141
Establishing whether there is room for expansion 142
Feeding 143
Hefting 143
Using other feeds and applications 143
Swarming and supersedure 144
Marking a queen 147
Collecting honey 147
Returning the frames 149

Chapter 22: Bee Diseases **151**
Problems with bee genetics 152
Why bees contract diseases 152
Varroa 153
Foul brood 158
Small hive beetle (*aethina tumida*) 159
Nosema 160
Wax moths 161
Chalkbrood 161
Stone brood 161
Tracheal mites 162
Viral infections 162
Sacbrood 162
Chilled Brood 163

Index 163

CHAPTER 1

INTRODUCTION TO CHICKENS, DUCKS AND BEES

You choose a noble undertaking when you decide to grow some of your own food. I get excited about food and where it comes from; you might even say I am obsessed with it. There is something marvellous about growing something, caring for it, nurturing it and thence making something wonderful to eat or drink.

This was once the major occupation of every person in the country. The provision of food is rightly ingrained in our culture because it is the way we survive. In fact, more than survive – prosper, enjoy, delight in life. It is as true for growing vegetables as it is for keeping livestock.

This book is about people. It's about you, although it is supposed to be about chickens, ducks and bees – with a few extras thrown in, it is really about you and the relationship you have with your animals – and of course, it is about the way in which you care for them.

Whether you are keeping animals as pets or as a way of providing your family with food, this regime of care is your responsibility and therefore this book is more about you than anyone else.

KEEPING ANIMALS FOR FOOD

The world is changing. Actually, it is stopping changing – let me explain. Over two hundred years ago a process started in earnest to change the way people lived. Actually, this change originated a mile away from where I am sitting at my computer. Hargreaves' 'Spinning Jenny' made it possible for mill owners to create vast wealth out of the work of other men, and the Industrial Revolution began. From the turn of the eighteenth century, the movement of people from the land to the towns was huge. People were paid for their work in paper money, often with little value, and because they spent over half the day in the mill, they had no time for fundamental domestic tasks such as baking bread, growing vegetables, brewing beer. William Cobbett, an MP from Oldham, Lancashire, was so outraged by the change in the diet of ordinary people that he wrote a book, *Cottage Economy*, where the basics of food production were spelt out.

Eventually, Cobbett left the country because of his views and, as the Georgian period became the Victorian period, people whose great-grandparents were used to the best food in Europe were starving as wages fell time and again. The continuation of land reform that put all common land in the hands of the rich, and then the banks, made the translocation from the land for the ordinary person complete.

The improvement of people's diet was accomplished by importing cheap food from the Empire, a methodology used by most European countries. Indeed, the UK has never been self-sufficient in food since the Industrial Revolution.

Studies in universities around the world have highlighted the unsustainable nature of the continued importing of food to feed the large cities of the world, and that famine in future generations will more likely occur in western cities than in what we traditionally call the Third World. Consequently there is a need for two things above all else in our modern society – the need to grow food and the skills to cook it.

It is not wrong to want to keep animals for the food they provide, as well as their other benefits, such as keeping you in nutrient-rich soil to provide for your garden.

WHY TIMES ARE CHANGING

Because you are reading this book, you may be one of a growing number of people intent on living a simple lifestyle – that of self-sufficiency. It has been associated with crankiness of hippy lifestyles, but has become much more mainstream in recent years. If the studies are accurate, one thing is certain: every family in the UK will have to grow at least some of their own food.

WHY CHICKENS, DUCKS AND BEES?

There is a simple answer to this: these are the animals you are allowed to keep in your gardens or on allotments without having to have a holding number issued by the Government. You can add to this rabbits, but they are outside the remit of this book. Certainly, goats and pigs, as well as sheep, need a holding number, and the reason for this is mostly down to animal welfare and the containment of diseases like foot and mouth.

This doesn't mean that you are completely free to keep chickens, ducks or bees. Your house deeds, the local authority or the local parish byelaws might forbid the keeping of animals of any kind at your address.

KEEPING ANIMALS WON'T SAVE YOU MONEY

Let me make this clear. Keeping animals will not, ever, save you money. It might bring you out (or nearly out) of the money economy, but it won't actually make life cheaper, except in the provision of honey, which at the moment is so expensive that a single hive might earn you £300 in a good year and nothing at all in a bad one.

You will always be able to buy eggs more cheaply than you can produce them, and you will always be able to purchase chicken meat for less than you are able to produce it, for the time being at least.

The truth is that the chickens themselves have provided cheap eggs and meat by being forced into intolerable conditions in factory farms to provide you and me with cheap meat and eggs.

THREE GREAT REASONS FOR KEEPING ANIMALS

There are three good reasons for keeping livestock in your garden. First, you get great food – eggs are so much more wonderful, for example, when cooked within minutes of coming out of a hen than the month-old examples you buy from the supermarkets.

Second, livestock is wonderful as a part of an overall strategy for being more self-sufficient. Ducks in particular vacuum up slugs and snails, bees provide a crop from the whole of your neighbourhood, and chickens provide mountains of manure to feed your vegetables.

Third, they are great fun. Only when you have studied life in the beehive can you find real insights into human behaviour. Your family benefits not only from healthy, wonderful, fresh, pesticide-free food, but they will have an insight into the natural world so frequently missed in modern life.

TEACUP PHILOSOPHY

It is difficult not to become something of a philosopher when you keep livestock of any kind. If you want to become proficient at the job, you have to spend time watching your animals, and consequently you will see, or maybe imagine, that the animals in your charge will have philosophies of their own. Whether this is pure imagination or not doesn't really matter, because your livestock will continue to live in their way regardless of what you or I think about them.

In essence, keeping animals for food says more about you as a human being than it does about a chicken being a chicken. She will cluck away, demanding food and clean water, somewhere dry and airy to sleep and a place to lay her eggs. These things never change, but you will notice some amazing transformations.

For example, how magical is it that a handful of pellets is transformed into an egg each day? Eggs and a small mountain of poo! The rate of return is quite fantastic too, since chickens seem to be a super-efficient food-converting machine. You notice this with bees, too, who forage out there and create the most exciting array of products, where huge numbers of insects, each intent on doing its bit for the colony, produce an amazing bounty.

How I wish we as humans lived like bees. Less enlightened beekeepers sometimes say bees live a little like us. Well, it is a point of view, but in many ways bees are our superiors. Quite unlike humans, they have no overall ruler, daily tasks are not decided by committee; they simply see and do according to their instinct, but here there is reason to see cycles in the pattern of life of a bee colony. Its numbers grow and subside according to the seasons; they reproduce, like so many animals, mostly in the spring; they are born and die in strict cyclic repetition and their organisation within the colony provides for the continued existence of the species.

The study of the bee provides plenty of examples of where mankind's action is both short-sighted and plainly wrong. You will not find in this book the 'Paul Peacock' method of best beekeeping. What you will find is the standard, because from there you will be able to move on and develop your own interaction with bees. But you will also find questions. For example, if bees have lived on the earth since flowers appeared – around 120 million years (or thereabouts) – and have evolved their own behaviour that suits the particular locality, why do we think we are better than all that evolution?

BECOMING MORE SELF-SUFFICIENT

Becoming more self-sufficient is entirely in keeping with the idea of this book, since hens, ducks and bees are part of a wider, more self-sufficient lifestyle. Whatever we say about getting a smallholding and some land, most of us will never, ever, get anywhere near this idyll but we can all do something in our gardens to make us more self-sufficient.

The need to become more self-sufficient is becoming more and more important. For example, the Incas lived in the biggest cities in the world, and they died out because they ran out of food. The Babylonian and Asia Minor cities each died out because of a lack of food. So could the same thing happen to us? That is why it is so important to get into a culture of growing our own food and keeping some livestock.

CHAPTER 2

ORGANISING THE GARDEN FOR LIVESTOCK

Everyone has their dreams. Mine has been to completely remove myself from humanity, except for my beautiful wife and produce lots of fat babies who live off the products of the land I have, the vegetables I grow and the animals I keep. Unfortunately, that remains a dream, though my wife is beautiful and my children are not fat, but healthy.

Like all countrymen of my class, I have no land to speak of, certainly not enough of it to enable me to be totally self-sufficient. Consequently, I am a wage slave and only have modest means to produce my own food. Fitting it all in is difficult; trying to combine poultry with vegetables is particularly difficult so the successful urban smallholder has to be organised and clever.

Land is at a premium, and since what I grow is particularly important to me, I have to make sure my livestock doesn't gobble the lot.

FINDING OUT ALL YOU CAN BEFORE BUYING YOUR LIVESTOCK

I bought my first hens at an auction. They were a mixed bag of good layers, hopelessly old birds, flighty bantams and what not. I didn't understand them, but muddled my way through, probably breaking the law in the way I transported them from the market to the allotment.

It was spring. All the allotments were marked out, green shooting cabbages and onions were tasting the splendid summer sunshine and everyone on their respective plots was eagerly awaiting the summer's growth. My newly bought hens had their own ideas.

No one had told me – but this is no excuse and I should have found out – that hens could fly over a six-foot fence. Consequently, I nearly lost the plot (literally) as the red-faced Hon. Secretary tore a strip off me because my birds were growing fat on everyone's seedlings.

My apology was only just enough, and there followed a frantic wing-clipping session. Before you plan, get some knowledge to begin with, and you will save yourself heartache.

HENS

Allow about 2 square metres as a minimum (an absolute minimum) run for the hens, and have enough space to move them around every three months but 10 square metres per hen if they are to be free-range. There is nothing to stop you making your run the same size as a raised bed, and when you have finished give your hens some time on that bed. They will manure it for you and eat the slugs, etc., scratching away with enthusiasm.

Your hens produce food and manure, and you will want to compost this rich material. Composting will be mentioned elsewhere in this book, but you should have a double-bin system for best results. Fill bin 1 which will then start to rot down. Once this is full tip it into bin 2 to complete the job. If it takes you six months to fill bin 1 then the rest of the year it will be rotting in bin 2. This allows you to fill bin 1 again while the rest of the compost is rotting.

A double-bin system needs 2 square metres, and is static. The bins are a metre high and you can make them from pallets.

The hen hutch should face east–west if possible, allowing you the best of winter sunshine, and make shade in the summer by growing crops such as runner beans along its side.

You can keep the hens off your crops in a number of ways. First, keep them locked into their run in the mornings. This forces them to get their full ration of layers' pellets for a good diet. Over the years I have developed a system of raised beds which will conveniently house either a horticultural fleece covering or a mini polytunnel covering. The fleece provides for an even temperature inside – but less wind. You can water through it, and of course, you can build it so no insects will get inside and spoil your crops. This has to be the ideal organic gardening material, and it will also keep the hens off your crops. They will jump on the fleece from time to time with such alarming consequences to them as the world gives way beneath them, that they probably won't bother again.

DUCKS

Organisationally, ducks are like hens in every respect except for more water. A careful study of commercial – so-called 'free-range' duck accommodation – makes the point that they only need to be able to wash their faces to be happy. This is because ducks get sticky eyes. However, I am personally happier if they can also get their bottoms in the water and have a splash. They look so happy as they scrabble about, so there must be some merit in having a small pond. It only needs to be a small pond, though, as you are not trying to recreate the village green.

For many years I used a sunken baby bath – enough for two birds to splash around in and not so deep as to kill a hen should she fall in. You also need to protect children – so have a plan!

The key is not to let the water become stagnant or dirty. It needs to be changed every day or two so there is constant fresh water available to the ducks – the discarded can be tipped onto your crops, so it's not wasted.

BEES

Preparing for bees takes care and time. A lot of people think bees are bound to swarm and cause all kinds of trouble. That might be the case – but rarely is. With planning you can avoid most swarming needs of the colonies and raise your bees so no one even knows they are there.

Bees should be kept out of direct sunlight, away from icy winds in the winter and driving rain. I have kept bees in the middle of housing estates and the only clue to their whereabouts was me looking like a chain-smoking idiot in my bee suit and smoker – walking down the garden path.

Your bees can be made more or less invisible if you force them to climb upward over a high obstacle. Point the hive entrance away from most of the general populace and surround it with a hedge or fence eight feet high and no one will ever know there are bees in the area.

The trick comes in your second year, when you might want to increase your colonies, and you then have 120,000 bees in the garden in the summer. My usual response to this is to place my bees somewhere else. Often you can talk to a farmer, but even a public park might – with permission – have some out-of-the-way place for bees.

Look around and think about siting your bees away from prying eyes and possible harm.

One last point before you turn to the beekeeping chapters: join your local beekeeping society! Not only will your membership provide insurance, there will also be many people who are more than able – and willing – to accommodate your hive.

PART ONE
CHICKENS

CHAPTER 3

INTRODUCTION TO CHICKENS

THE HEN AND WHAT SHE NEEDS

Hens are wonderful, curious, exciting, lovable, tough, intelligent, resourceful, productive, thrifty, communal, clean animals that are relatively easy to care for, generally disease free and, so long as you take care of them, will provide food, interest and amusement for many years.

Thinking about keeping poultry is frequently brought into sharp focus if you consider the Five Freedoms. These are the brainchild of the Farm Animal Welfare Council who consider that good animal welfare implies both fitness and a sense of well-being. Any animal kept by man must, at least, be protected from unnecessary suffering. The Five Freedoms are:

1. **Freedom from hunger and thirst** – by ready access to fresh water and a diet to maintain full health and vigour.

2. **Freedom from discomfort** – by providing an appropriate environment, including shelter and a comfortable resting area.

3. **Freedom from pain, injury or disease** – by prevention or rapid diagnosis and treatment.

4. **Freedom to express normal behaviour** – by providing sufficient space, proper facilities and company of the animal's own kind.

5. **Freedom from fear and distress** – by ensuring conditions and treatment which avoid mental suffering.

The ability to supply all of these is the starting point for a happy relationship between you and your animals. The concept of the Five Freedoms originated with the *Report of the Technical Committee to Enquire into the Welfare of Animals Kept under Intensive Livestock Husbandry Systems*, the Brambell Report, published in December 1965. This stated that farm animals should have freedom 'to stand up, lie down, turn around, groom themselves and stretch their limbs', a list that is still sometimes referred to as Brambell's Five Freedoms.

These freedoms are not to be the absolute rule of your animal welfare routine because you cannot always keep animals in full health; they sometimes get sick. An ill hen does not automatically mean you have failed it somehow. Keeping hens at all, especially if they have come from a cage, is doing hen-kind a real service.

HAVING TIME TO LOOK AFTER YOUR HENS

On the one hand you cannot be too busy to keep hens. They love being let out in the morning, fed and watered as necessary, then left to their own devices (so long as they are safe) until you return home to gaze away the pressures of the day. On the other hand, however, you can often think they live in the same fashion as we do: rush, skip meals, get too excited, forgetful and panic-stricken under the pressures of modern life. You must not forget to provide your hens with the needs of the day: food, water, protection and shelter from weather and predators.

You need to plan the purchase of good quality food, and not let a day go by without a good supply.

To keep hens is to be always prepared for their needs and your ability to keep the regime going. Indeed, as I write this, I notice it is going dark and my birds will need locking up – so I'm off to say 'goodnight'. Should I not manage this, tonight could just be the night the fox gets them, or the driving wind and rain make a real mess of their sleeping arrangements.

To say the hen is a machine that converts all kinds of food, from the pellets we give them as their daily ration to the worms, insects, roots and shoots they scrabble on their daily transit around the garden into a daily egg would be understating the point.

As well as the daily egg, they give us a great amount of pleasure.

EATING THE MEAT

For anyone intent on self-sufficiency chickens raised for meat are possibly the most luxurious foods you can have. You know the quality of the food that has gone into them and can guarantee a wonderful life for the chicken. In the old days people used to (and clearly still do) keep a lot of hens and eat those which had gone through their second stage of laying eggs, more of which later. It would mean keeping two flocks, and constantly rearing replacements. The hens would be eaten at the same rate as their replacements would be available, and in the days before freezers, they would be despatched one by one as the needs of the family determined.

Of course, these days, hens can be dispatched, dressed and cleaned and popped in the freezer, which in my case is a fantastic way of separating the killing from the eating. When taking a hen for the table, or even when euthanising a hen on health grounds, I always feel like I will never eat meat again. But after a few days I have no qualms on taking a bird from the freezer.

USING THE FEATHERS

The number of things you can do with feathers is amazing. My favourite is the building of walls from concrete or mud, using feathers as a binding agent. But from the fishing fly to the stuffed pillow, those feathers are useful.

At the very least you can compost feathers. They make great absorbers of liquid in the compost heap, and rot down quite successfully.

One final use for them is stuffing in your bee smoker – I don't burn just feathers, but they do give off smoke.

ENJOYING FUN AND COMPANIONSHIP

I spend hours watching my hens. They are funny, complete characters in their own right, and they enjoy being alive. I enjoy looking after them. They give you something to care for, and they reward you by entering into your family, your flock.

For the price of a handful of layers' pellets, you have all the entertainment you need. Studying them is an all-engrossing part of the day, and their robust nature means there are few sadnesses compared to the years of enjoyment.

On top of this, you can show your birds and get involved with numerous societies dedicated to poultry. The Poultry Club of Great Britain has a lot of local associations, where you can not only engage in social activities but get a lot of help and information too.

CLEARING UP POO

The chicken is a poo machine. You get lots of the stuff, and if you are a gardener, you will be very glad of it too! If you allow them free range around the garden, apart from having to net your crops, you have to be prepared to wash away poo from the paths. Hens produce a lot of poo at night, and you will be surprised how much you have to clean up. Of course, clearing poo is the worst of all the jobs, so once you are used to that, the rest of it is easy.

ENJOYING NEW-LAID EGGS

This is the major reason people buy hens. There is nothing on the planet better than having eggs that have come directly from the chicken – all other eggs will seem inferior. The shop-bought egg is usually up to a month old, and vastly reduced in quality compared to the very minute it was laid. Your new-laid egg has all its membranes intact. This means the yolk sits tight and the white doesn't flow all over the pan.

You are entering egg lover's heaven, when you first get hens.

I once collected all the eggs in the hutch and replaced them with eggs that had little lions on them. When a certain person, whose name shall be omitted to save her blushes, went to collect eggs for a recipe to put in one of her baking books, it caused considerable confusion.

You can find out a lot about your hens from the state of the eggs. Thin, bloodied, poo covered, double yolked, or without a shell at all, each of these symptoms relates to problems with the hen.

WHAT DO YOUR CHICKENS NEED?

At the most basic level chickens need a balanced food ration, clean water, somewhere to escape from the rain and cold, and a safe roosting point, safe from predators. Consequently, keeping hens in cages in sheds, though in my opinion a shameful way to keep animals, does keep hens in prime health – though at a cost.

But to keep hens in the garden, on the allotment or anywhere on grass, produces a number of problems that we will look at in more detail in later chapters. Mites, worms and mud are the first set of problems and then there are problems among hens – pecking, bullying and overly randy cockerels all have to be dealt with.

Finally, broodiness can cause problems if you don't want a high number of chicks, but can be fantastic if you wish to bring up your own flock. Hens go broody at almost any time, and will sit on a clutch of eggs that they will defend with ferocious stabbing pecks. Hens become bad-tempered and useless for anything other than keeping these eggs warm.

Mostly you will need to discourage the hen from being broody. A number of techniques work, but there are no guarantees. Some techniques that you should certainly not try include plunging the hen into freezing water – the poor thing would probably not survive it, neither would it be fair to confine the animal in an upturned bucket, a remedy shared with me by an Irish farmer in a pub. He was all secrets, 'Come 'ere sir, I have a great tip for you.' I have to confess I thought it was a horse tip he was giving me. He said he had a dozen broody hens in buckets, each with a brick on to stop them wandering around.

The breed can affect the broodiness of the animal. As you would imagine, modern egg farms do not really need broody hens, and the 'little brown hybrids' they use are almost completely non-broody.

DO YOU NEED A COCKEREL?

In truth hens do prefer life when there is a cockerel around. He orders his flock, defends them and mates regularly with them, too. If you have more than one cockerel, you will get fighting, or at least competition. You can separate flocks, each having a cockerel but, especially if you live in the town, or have neighbours who like their early mornings unadulterated by loud crowings, hens do just as well without a cockerel at all. Town hens do not need a cockerel, and you get just as many eggs, as well as happy neighbours.

WHERE TO PUT YOUR HENS

It is possible to keep hens in a garden – even a backyard is good enough, but there are some restrictions and things you need to remember.

You have to move the hens around the garden so the soil they are running on does not build up parasites. This means the hutch and any associated run must be moveable. Their scratching and patting will ruin a patch of grass within a couple of days, leaving you with bare earth. Very fertile, but very bare earth.

Be sure the run is as predator-proof as possible, and if you can let them loose in the garden, your fences need to be chicken-proof, because otherwise they will find a way out of the garden if they can.

You need about 100 metres square (that is 10 metres by 10 metres) for each free-range hen, but they don't need all that space in one sitting (if you'll excuse the pun). You can restrict your hens so they are still able to behave like hens. Don't overcrowd them, as this leads to bullying. You are not starting a hen farm in the back garden, you are keeping a few hens, maybe enough to be self-sufficient in eggs – so don't try to have too many.

Move your hens every two to three months and don't put them back on the same land for at least three months. This keeps the parasite load to a minimum, as natural forces, other animals and lack of food for the predators will reduce their number.

HOUSING YOUR HENS

Housing is probably the most important aspect of all. Hens take themselves to bed at night and much prefer to sleep on a branch like perch. They feel safe high up and, if necessary, they can fly out of danger. Your hutch and any associated run needs to be predator-safe. More than anything your run needs to be dry, well ventilated but draught free, regularly cleaned and checked for red mite, and cleared for the same.

There should be more than one nest box, especially if you have more than two hens, to cut down the competition for laying space.

It is usually best to have water available in the hutch, but I personally prefer also to keep food and a supply of water outside.

SITING THE HUT

The hut is best placed out of direct sunlight, out of wind and too much rain. Though hens do need to have plenty of light, dappled shade is perfect. The hut needs to be easily ventilated in hot weather, but there is no need to insulate it in winter.

If you are able, put the hut floor off the ground, with at least 30 cm between the floor and the earth. This will stop mice and rats from nesting underneath – they don't like to be exposed in any way.

One last point, if you are on a hill, place the hut as high as possible. This ensures the soil is less waterlogged in winter (mud is a real problem). If you have a serious problem with mud, consider keeping the hens on paving slabs. You can cover the slabs with bark, compost or even soil, so the hens can scratch away, but you should be able to clear away this material (with any associated parasites as well!).

SPARE HOUSING

The next thing you need to have in place is some way of separating the hens should there be a problem. If one hen is being bullied, for example, and fails to eat and drink, she will deteriorate very quickly and will need to be removed. Consequently, you need some way of housing her. This needn't be an elaborate affair – just a wooden box, which is waterproof, with a perch for the bird to climb on at night and a chicken wire frame for a small run.

STOPPING YOUR HENS FIGHTING

You should keep more than one bird: they are flock animals.

You will soon learn that hens are not human, and their habits are not like ours. If they are overcrowded or going into moult, or of different sizes they may fight. Bullying can be quite distressing and often leads to the death of one of the birds.

You can stop this by making sure they have enough room and are never able to fight once they start having a go. Keeping eggs collected is a good idea; don't let them build up in the nest box, and if there is ever a cracked egg, collect it straightaway. Once they taste egg, it can turn their heads quite easily.

TEMPERATURE

Hens evolved in hot countries, and rarely do they suffer from the heat in the UK, but from time to time the summertime temperature is hot enough, and the sun strong enough to give them heatstroke. They need shade in the summer, and plenty of water. In cases where the hen is panting and really suffering, it is best to douse them with water to get the heat out of them, and this usually works fine.

The opposite is just as bad. There are several days in the winter where the temperature is really cold. A night-time feed of corn is slowly digested, giving off heat to keep the animal from death's door overnight. Do not be tempted to use a greenhouse heater, which my friend once did, resulting in complete catastrophe and a stern letter from the RSPCA.

Everyone thinks the best way to stop water from freezing is to add salt, which is a problem for hens. By far the best way to keep water from freezing is to add some glycerine, the hens hardly notice it.

CLIPPING WINGS

A part of the process of keeping your hens low key is to be sure they don't fly over the fence and eat your neighbour's plants. So you will have to clip their wings. This is neither dangerous or painful, it is just like having your nails clipped.

You need a partner for this, especially if you have never done this before. You have to hold the bird firmly between your body and your arm, making sure the wing nearest your body isn't crumpled, or unable to be moved. Then you need to gently pull the other wing out.

Your partner then cuts just a few centimetres off the flight feathers, recognisable by their large size and central location. Don't cut too deep, the lower half of the feathers has nerve endings inside, and you can make them bleed – all you need is to cut the ends. You only need to cut one wing – if you try both, the effect is ruined.

Should the bird try to fly she gets differing lift from the newly cut wing and cannot control herself properly. She simply doesn't bother to fly, but can still use her wings in that fast, flapping run they use to escape trouble.

A WORD ABOUT SICKNESS

Before you keep hens you have to be sure that you know what to do if they get sick. When hens get sick it is usually because they have been badly fed, are being bullied by another hen, need worming, or they have some other parasitic problem such as red mite, or they may have caught one of the many diseases we still have no vaccine against. Buying hens from a reputable source will ensure they are full immunised.

By far the most common cause of poor health is poor feeding. It is amazing what people think hens eat – they try a light salad, or scraps from the table. They think they will do well on bread or cake, and it is surprising how many experienced poultry keepers think mixed corn is a decent ration for a hen.

The truth is that hens need layers' pellets. This is their main meal of the day and they should not really be allowed anything else until they have had their fill. Following this, they can be allowed to run around the garden to eat whatever, but nothing other than layers' pellets will keep them happy.

We will return to the question of feeding hens many times in the poultry section, as well as the others. You cannot overemphasise the importance of good feeding and how the health of your animals depends on it.

When they do get sick, you have to treat them and later on we will look more closely at the kind of diseases they get. But, before you get hens, hunt out a vet that knows something about them. This is important, because not all vets are good at hens, and you could just be wasting your money. This seems harsh, but if you go to your local vet and explain you are thinking of getting hens, and ask them whether they consider themselves a poultry practice, then they will advise you. Vets are as specialised as doctors, and when you consider the variety of animals they have to cope with, it is obvious some will be better at some than others.

WHAT DO HENS REALLY ENJOY?

Hens love to dust-bathe. They will find a dry spot and simply wallow, getting dust into their feathers, and if this is in dappled shade in the highest heat of the year they will be completely happy.

They also love to eat and drink together, their demeanour and behaviour communicates to each other their mood, health and status. The comb is a good way of recognising how the hens are doing. Pale combs might mean sickness, but could also mean the hens are young. As soon as they colour up the males know the bird is ready for mating.

Hens have a strong sexual drive, it is how they have become successful over the ages.

CHECKING THAT YOU HAVE PERMISSION TO KEEP HENS

The various things you are going to have to buy or erect in order to keep hens will be dealt with in other chapters. However, it is worth taking a minute to look into the vexed question of the permissions needed to keep hens.

We have seen the sad news stories where people have had their hens removed from their property because they didn't have permission to keep them. This is because either they are in breach of their tenancy agreement or some local byelaw, or their deeds strictly forbid the keeping of livestock.

You need to check your situation before you buy, because if someone complains, you will need to be prepared.

Do your deeds prevent you from keeping livestock?

About 10% of the private homes in the country have a clause stating livestock of any kind cannot be kept in the garden. There is usually no way to get round this, but should you go ahead and keep hens, my advice would be to keep them in ultra-hygienic conditions, being 'on the ball' with their care, and sweeten your neighbours with the odd box of eggs.

Council tenants

Usually there is a proviso in your tenancy agreement that no livestock are allowed on council property, but this relates really to the keeping of horses, sheep and other livestock. Beyond this there is usually an understanding that a few hens is fine so long as they are not causing a nuisance. There are still people who keep pigeons, rabbits, guinea pigs and ferrets in their gardens, and these are also covered by the same agreements.

In essence the situation for the council tenant is similar to the allotment holder, where a small number of hens are still allowed for by law. But, should your hens get out of hand by entering other gardens and eating their prize dahlias, increase to an unacceptable number, or make a constant din at 3 a.m. in the summer, you are likely to find yourself in trouble.

Private tenants

Here, almost exclusively, you are at the mercy of your landlord. If they say no, there is usually nothing you can do. Be sure, should you decide to keep hens, to be able to demonstrate they are no trouble, they are clean and perfectly in keeping with the house and its gardens. And be sure to be able to place them elsewhere if you are ordered to remove them in a rush.

DISPATCHING YOUR HENS

On the whole, chickens are robust animals. There is no reason why your hens should not live much longer than five years as a minimum. I think the oldest hen is about 20 years old, and still lays the odd egg. However, hens can get sick and die, too. The most important thing you can do as a first step to good hen health is to find a vet who has considerable poultry experience. As I said earlier, don't be afraid to ask around.

The other important thing to learn is how to dispatch your hen should you need to. If you are going to eat your hens, learning how to kill by dislocation is important, and is probably best to be taught by a proficient person.

This is what the law says: for commercial killing of any animal, you have to use the stun/bleed method. This involves touching the head with an electrode, then once the animal is stunned, slitting a vein in the neck. This causes the animal to die from loss of blood. If you need to kill poultry only singly for home consumption or for humane reasons, you are allowed to kill by dislocation of the neck.

Under no circumstances should you attempt to chop the animal's head off. This is illegal and dangerous. Neither should you use the old method of a notched-out broom handle, which frequently results in the bird suffering stress and the head coming right off.

The so-called 'killing cone' that looks like a megaphone in which the bird is placed head down and killed with a type of pliers is also not allowed, even for a one-off killing.

The rules governing animal welfare at slaughter and killing are set down in Directive 93/119/EC on the protection of animals at the time of slaughter or killing and implemented in Great Britain by the Welfare of Animals (Slaughter or Killing) Regulations 1995 (WASK) and in Northern Ireland by the Welfare of

Animals (Slaughter or Killing) Regulations (Northern Ireland) 1996.

GETTING ADVICE

As with most things in the human world, you will get different advice from different poultry keepers. You need advice, really before you start, if only to boost your confidence. Look around a number of suppliers, and go to some people who you know will be able to help you – maybe someone at your local allotment keeps poultry. Look in the newspaper for local members of The Poultry Club of Great Britain and perhaps go on a course. Most poultry suppliers run courses about poultry-keeping too, and this will give you the confidence you need to start keeping chickens.

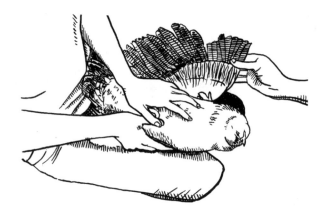

CHAPTER 4

HANDLING YOUR HENS

This is quite an important subject. It is important to handle your hens for the reasons below. At the same time you have to realise that even if you bought your hens from a reputable source, you cannot be 100% sure they are free from disease. Make sure you wear an overall or something and gloves to protect your clothes from infection which you might accidentally transfer to your insides later on.

Children in particular can be susceptible to salmonella, and although your hens should have been immunised, just as when you bought them you would think twice about eating a raw egg, you should have similar caution with the birds themselves.

Always make sure you wash your hands and that your tetanus injections are up to date. A nasty peck could have all kinds of consequences. If you are allowing children to hold your hens, don't let them do it unsupervised.

WHY WOULD YOU WANT TO HOLD YOUR HENS?

There are many reasons for regularly holding your hens. First of all, if one becomes sick, and you have to examine the bird, you will not be increasing its stress if it is already used to being handled. If a sick bird that normally runs away from you actually needs to be picked up and placed in a carry box to visit the vet, the ordeal can be very stressful to the point of being dangerous.

Regular handling of your hens is an important part of their regime of care. This way you can clip wings, administer all kinds of treatments, such as flea and mite powder and generally clean them up.

The regime involves the following.

▶ No kissing

Please don't kiss your hens. They don't appreciate it and probably think you are trying to bite them. I suppose if you are going to kiss them anywhere, it will be around the top of the head, and therefore you open yourself up to a jolly good pecking, which will leave you with health worries.

▶ No handling around the bottom (unless you need to)

This should only be done in very specific circumstances. You should avoid poo as a backdrop at all times if possible. A trick to find out if the hen is near the point of lay is to place your fingers between the hip bones near the bottom. If you can get two fingers there, the animal will soon be laying.

▶ Always wash afterwards

Without exception, you should wash your hands, and anything else for that matter, after handling hens or their eggs, or cleaning out the hut. Use an antibacterial soap and hot water but be mindful you don't scald yourself.

► Change your clothes
It is better still to have special clothes to wear when you are going to handle your birds. This can act as a stimulus for the birds – whenever they see you in a white overall, they know they are going to be picked up, and will often come to you to get some food. Special clothes can include neoprene gloves and glasses, especially for children, who are more liable to be a victim of a scratching, panicking bird.

► Have a tetanus shot if necessary, if you have been scratched
Birds scratch in the soil, where tetanus is found. If they scratch you – well, you get the idea.

► No chasing
You will get nowhere by chasing your birds around the garden. They will never come to you but rather stress out every time they see you. They will become nervous birds and you will wear yourself out running around the garden.

Take your time when you collect your birds. Talk to them in gentle tones and hold out food for them to take. Do not use sudden movements but have a calm demeanour and they will come to you.

► Hens are not pets
You might own these birds, but they are not pets, in that their purpose for living is not to be petted. They might never get used to being handled, and run away whenever they see you trying to pick them up. You have to spend time earning the right to handle them.

Crouch beside them, making short, soft repetitive sounds, holding food and generally maintaining what they consider a safe distance from them. Leave the food on the ground and then walk away. This may need to be repeated several times before they start coming near you.

Mating: Seizing the opportunity

Hens that have no cockerel will frequently treat you as their mate, squatting down into a mating position every time you go by. Take the opportunity to pick them up each time they do this and you will find them easy to handle. Talk to them, gently stroke them for 30 seconds and then gently put them down after around 30 seconds, and if you can, leave them a little food.

HOW TO HOLD A HEN

This can be done in many ways. Personally I am not a fan of holding them by the legs or by the wings. It can be uncomfortable for them and they will respond to this, becoming resistant to handling. They frequently open their wings, making it harder for them to move around without banging them. Holding them by the wings (sort of under their armpits) is very uncomfortable for them.

I prefer to hold the hen in a comfortable stance, using my body to hold one wing still, and my arm to hold the other, in a firm but easy grip. This way, should they struggle and try to flap their wings, they will not be able to do so, and consequently will damage neither themselves nor yourself. The other benefit of this method is that you usually have a free hand to do whatever you have to do with the bird.

Using a partner

Some operations need two people and you need to plan for this.

Wing clipping is a case in point. One person holds the animal in place against the body and arm and at a comfortable point opens out the wing to be clipped. The other person takes about 3 to 4 cm off the tips of the flight feathers.

RELEASING YOUR HEN

Don't think, because they are birds, you can throw them onto the grass to land with much flapping and much 'bok-bokking'. They need to be placed down as easily as possible, and this means changing your grip so you are holding them in both your hands.

This way they can walk off with no distress and will simply ruffle a little, and walk away. If you are able, give them some food as a treat.

USING A CARRY BOX

Taking your hen to the vet, or moving it anywhere, should be done in a specially-made hen carrier. These are basically sturdy, hen-sized carrier boxes that allow no real view of the outside. You need to be sure the hen can fit into and out of the box correctly and comfortably, without it having to bend around small entrances. Cat and dog boxes will not do – you need a lid at the top so you can hold the wings firmly.

Talk to your birds, making comforting sounds to them so they feel less afraid, and get used to talking to them as you handle them. If possible the bird should be fed and watered before it is transported.

Drive carefully and slowly to avoid throwing the hen and its box around the car, and remember to leave the hen to rest motionless before taking it out of the box. It might not like to go back into the box, so prepare yourself for some resistance.

CHAPTER 5

HOW TO FEED HENS

A national newspaper wrote in the summer of 2010 that anyone could keep hens as all they need to live on is kitchen scraps. Nothing could be further from the truth. If you feed your hens on kitchen scraps you will find yourself with sick hens on your hands. Of course, they will scratch about the garden and provide themselves with a fairly well-balanced diet, but you would be amazed at what people think they eat!

One lady called into a radio phone-in programme about sick hens, and was asked what she was feeding them. 'A nice salad', she said with some pride. Another fed them sausages, another eggs, another collected snails and slugs for them, yet another fed them Kellogg's Corn Flakes.

The most important part of being a chicken is getting the right food to eat. A hen's diet is complex, and there are some obvious reasons for it. First, a laying hen needs a lot of calcium in the diet; she cannot make shells from nothing. Then the bird produces a lot of protein in the form of albumen in the white of the egg and a lot of fat and minerals in the yolk. Her diet needs to reflect this, as well as provide all the various nutrients and energy for the everyday nutrition of the body. In order to keep herself going the hen is constantly pecking at possible food.

The fundamental basic food for a hen is a combination of grain, oils and proteins bought by the hen-keeper in a complete ration to match the age and development of the hen.

There is a wonderful 1940s book called *Raising Hens and Rabbits on Kitchen Scraps*, a great necessity during war time, although you were provided with a ration of grain for each hen to supplement their diet. However, on starting out in hen-keeping you must understand: hens need the right food, and we will repeat this time and again. Good food means healthy hens.

THE IMPORTANCE OF PROTEIN

Young hens need protein to grow, and this needs to be in their food. From hatching to six weeks, the crumbs fed to chicks, called starters' ration, can be up to 20% protein. From six weeks to 14 weeks the ration changes to 'growers' ration' which is around 17% protein.

Beyond this you find 'layers' ration' which is around 15% protein, covering all the hen's needs for day-to-day adult life.

Feeding cockerels, you might think, should be easier, because they do not produce eggs. However, they do produce a lot of sperm. If the cockerel is covering half a dozen hens, he will be delivering much more high protein material than his courtesan's egg-a-day equivalent.

Fundamentally, your hens need their ration, starters' ration, growers' ration and layers' ration as their main diet. Everything else is an extra, whether it be grass, insects and grubs, bits of bread, cabbages (which they love), worms; all these should be considered an addition to the ration rather than the basic daily diet.

Hens are not greedy

Unlike dogs and small boys, hens will not eat and eat until they explode. Consequently a hopper system is a convenient way of providing pellets. You can be sure they will not eat their way through all the food at once.

THE BEST WAYS OF DELIVERING FOOD

Whenever you see an old rural film there is almost always someone somewhere in a farmyard throwing a few handfuls of grain to a gallop of chasing hens. It is a cute idea, but not practical unless you happen to have a farmyard and a small army of ferocious cats to frighten off the rats and mice that would also be attracted to the scattered food.

For the most practical poultry feeding it is best to use some kind of trough or a hopper delivery system.

FEEDING HENS IN THE CITY

It is important, in the city, to be able to show your neighbours that there is nothing to worry about in relation to rats. Consequently it is best to keep your feed locked away, at some distance from the hens, so rats cannot get to know it is there. Rats are intelligent animals, and have good memories. If they learn where the feed is kept, they will soon enough find a way of getting to it. With full bellies, you can be sure they will be looking to settle down in the neighbourhood, and before you know it they will be found wobbling across your neighbour's washing line and performing their particular form of high jinks around home and garden.

The first sight of a rat can cause 'chicken wars' between otherwise perfectly hospitable people, and you should go all out to be sure this doesn't arise.

Keeping food locked away, and feeding with a hopper that you take away each evening should be enough to keep the rat population more interested in other sources of human waste, of which there are plenty. But it's no good telling the people who live near you the rats came from somewhere else. They are your responsibility if they are sharing your chickens' food.

PELLETS OR MASH

Most people buy pellets for their birds because these flow more easily in a hopper delivery system, and they don't blow away if put into a trough. However, you can also buy the same product in a mash form, made of flakes. Mash is easier for small birds to eat, and you can make a wet mash from them. However, most hens do perfectly well on pellets.

One use for mash is to add this in a special food (see below) where the mash is combined with other foods.

USING A GRAVITY FEEDER

I have seen many of these, from small bought ones which hold a week's worth of feed to large DIY affairs, made from a dustbin and hung from the roof of a shed, holding at least a month or two's worth of food. They can be free-standing on the floor or they can be hung from a beam.

Either way, they need to be protected from the rain, otherwise the pellets go rotten at the delivery end and the whole thing clogs up. They come in two parts: a bucket or hopper, and a serving lid. You fill the bucket, and then attach the lid. Turn the whole feeder upside down and the hopper then loads the serving tray. As the birds eat their ration, the tray is re-filled.

Pros and cons

On the one hand the gravity feeder represents an easy way of feeding your birds for a week. If you have it hanging off the ground, it can be adjusted so your birds can peck away easily, but rats will find it impossible to reach.

If you use small feeders, and have many birds feeding from them, you could find the weaker birds being bullied in the general competition for space, so make sure you have enough feeders for birds to be able to eat away from bullying females. If you can separate the feeders from each other by around 5–10 metres, the hens will have a chance to feed and escape their rivals should they have any.

All hens are messy eaters, and you get food over the floor, which has to be cleaned up, and certain hens – the type that pushes food to the side – will make a terrible mess with a gravity feeder, wasting more than they eat.

The gravity feeder is not an opportunity to leave the hens unattended, even though is certainly more convenient.

PROVIDING WATER FOR YOUR HENS

There are basically two ways of watering hens: a trough or gravity watering.

In much the same way as gravity feeders work, an upturned bucket for water is a very convenient way of watering your birds. Hens are quite messy and will think nothing of pooing in their water, so the gravity feeder is beneficial because there is a comparatively small lip. You do have to keep your eye on this, and provide them with fresh water at least daily, and be prepared to clean the water trough or feeder if soiled.

The same goes for bullying with the water as does the food, so make sure you have a couple of places for birds to visit. It is best you clean the containers out very regularly, inside the buckets of the gravity feeder can get a layer of mucous quite easily, and troughs get very messy too. Why give your birds water you wouldn't wish to drink yourself?

Apple Cider Vinegar

About once a week I add a few tablespoons of Apple Cider Vinegar (ACV) to the water, which has a beneficial effect on the hens. Do it for a week every month, at a rate of about 20 ml to each litre. Many poultry keepers say it cures everything, which certainly it doesn't. However, you will find a weekly dose brings your hens a new lease of life.

Certainly it counteracts many parasites in the gut, and increases the acidity, helping to control worms, though it is not a substitute for a good worming. It is full of trace elements, minerals and vitamins. You will notice brighter feathers, a better comb and more alert hens.

Some people say ACV increases egg production, which is questionable, but it might mean fewer lost days in egg production.

PROVIDNG CALCIUM IN YOUR HENS' DIET

Hens produce eggs, and each egg has a shell. The minerals needed for good shell production include calcium and there should always be an excess available in hens' diet. Layers' pellets are a daily ration, but if you provide the hens with a pot of crushed shell, too, they will benefit doubly.

In the digestion of food, hens (like all birds) use grit to grind their food. Shell is an important source of grit, and they will get more benefit from their food when crushed shell is available. Also, some of the calcium is absorbed, making their egg shells stronger.

Under no circumstances should you feed their own eggshells back to the hens. This can cause them to peck at eggs, which in turn can lead to other problems such as bullying – a tortuous route that we shall explain later.

HOW MUCH DO CHICKENS EAT?

Chicks will eat about a kilo of food each in their first six weeks of life. This gives you a good guide on how much food to buy if you are starting off with chicks.

Adult birds eat differing amounts depending on the breed, the weather and if they are laying. They will obviously eat more if they are free-range rather than in a cage, and this also will depend on how much they can supplement their food.

Generally a hen will consume at least 25 g of feed a day plus 'extras'. We have already mentioned, but it is worth mentioning again, the importance of your hens eating their daily ration before filling up on other foods. It is worthwhile noting how much your hens are actually eating by taking careful notes over a week per month. This will give you an indicator when the amounts drop. Besides, it is pleasant to watch your hens and understand their ways.

PROVIDING 'EXTRAS'

It is possible to make mashes of various kinds. Boil up some potatoes and mash them. Add to this half as much layers' mash, maybe a couple of slices of bread and some chopped garlic. This can be served warm to the hens (but not hot) on a cold day. They will love it! The garlic is there to help digestion and possibly help with the parasite load. It is not a replacement for a worming regime.

The addition of some cabbage, sprouts tops and onion greens will also make for an extra special treat. However, although they will happily go around eating their way through your garden, try not to give them garden cuttings and general garden waste. Chickens know what they like to eat, and also what is bad for them, and you might be disguising something they wouldn't normally eat.

Although they are omnivores, try not to give them meat in their diet. Let them get their own in the form of insects, spiders and worms. It is not desirable to leave meat around the hutch or run, as it is sure to attract rats. Keep hens, so far as the food you give them is concerned, on a vegetarian diet – they'll do the rest.

A word about bread

We humans eat horrible bread as a rule. It is not food nutritious enough – the bread bought from the supermarket – to keep a hen alive, and even the very best bread isn't that good for them either.

By all means give them some bread to eat – they love it, but only once they have eaten their ration. Birds fed on bread alone go downhill rapidly and within a couple of days you will notice a difference for the worse.

Conclusion

Birds need the right food for their particular stage of development. Their basic, everyday, health-giving ration is layers' pellets. Make sure you clean up after them and store their food away from rats and mice.

CHAPTER 6

HOUSING HENS

You can find all kinds of housing, sometimes on garage forecourts, sometimes outside pet shops, greengrocers, enterprising florists and, increasingly, at garden centres. Much of the hen housing you find for sale is of inferior quality, fit for a year's worth of wear and easily holed by predators and vermin alike.

Of course, hens live in the wild too, where they exist in towns or the woodland edge, mostly in the Indian sub-continent. It is best to keep hens in such a way that mimics the environment they come from.

Hens need to feel safe, and consequently they perch up trees and on rooftops, away from mammalian predators. Housing should provide hens with this feeling of safety and have a perch for them to roost on. They have really strong grips, and will not fall off their roost even under the fiercest provocation.

Another thing is to give them room. If they have to compete for roosting space or nesting, they can fight, with distressing results. Don't overcrowd your hens and have at least one nest box per two to three hens.

Obviously, the more you spend on a hutch the better it is going to be, and don't rush into the purchase; make sure it is good, robust, and take time to shop around. Remember, your hens will spend a lot of time inside!

The first things you should think about when buying a hen hutch include:

▶ Can I clean it easily, and reach to all the corners, nooks and crannies?
▶ Are the materials robust enough to protect the hens from predators?

- ▶ Is the wood finished to such a standard that red mite can easily be dealt with?
- ▶ Are there sufficient nest boxes and are they comfortable?
- ▶ Are there nails and/or other problems (chicken wire is the worst) that might injure the hens or yourself?
- ▶ Are the roosts at a height to allow enough ventilation above the birds when sleeping?
- ▶ Is the roof leak-proof?
- ▶ Is the door sufficiently strong? (Badgers are enormously strong animals and will break through a door if they want to!)
- ▶ Is the hutch easily moveable?
- ▶ Is it possible to fit a run to the hutch to confine the birds, and, if so, is it easily removable?
- ▶ Can you access the nest boxes from the outside?
- ▶ Are you able to supply feed and water inside if the weather gets really, really bad?

The hutch is possibly one of the most important parts of a good health regime your hens can get. It is responsible for the quality of the air they breathe for large parts of the evening and the atmosphere inside the hut. Whether it is mites, bacteria, fungal spores or parasites in the poo, the amount of space they have, or the competition for roosting space, laying eggs or the ability to be able to escape bullying birds, the hutch is a very important piece of equipment.

PROVIDING VENTILATION

Birds in hutches are either too warm on hot summer evenings, or freezing in the darkest of winter nights. The rest of the time they are fine, unless it has been raining, when the birds spend the night drying out, steaming on their roosts.

First of all, ventilation is important because you don't want your birds breathing each other's breath too much. Too many birds in a hutch is dangerous because they can quickly infect each other, particularly when the weather is damp.

Many hutches are designed by dividing the roosting perch length by the assumed width of a hen. Very often a hut made for four birds really ought to have no more than three. If you imagine a sheet of A4 paper for each hen, then subtract 25%, you will have the comfortable stock for that particular hut.

MATERIALS

You will find two decidedly opposing camps in the chicken world: those who hate plastic and those who swear by it. The truth is many of these opposing views come from hutch manufacturers and are, I have to say, very persuasive in their arguments. However, a good plastic hutch is better than a bad wooden one, and vice versa. I have been very happy with a small plastic hutch made by a well-known British company. It has many design features that make it an excellent hut. Although it is advertised as being for four birds, I only keep two in it. This way ventilation is increased. It is often the same for wooden 'arks' which are essentially a triangle made of two sides and a floor.

Ventilation should come through shielded holes at the top of the hutch and not near the bottom. That way warm air from sleeping birds can escape from the hut. There are usually enough gaps in the bottom to allow a mild flow of replacement fresh air without enormous gales blasting through the hutch.

You get a lot of hen hutches made from material that is of inferior quality. Personally, I am not happy with huts made from what looks like 'waney lap' (thin, overlapping strips of wood, found in ubiqitous fences) boards or 3 mm ply because they either leak water up the joints or they are too flimsy to withstand a hit from a boot, football, lawn mower or a badger. (The fox is usually far too delicate to bash into things.) Often the floors of these huts are also made from flimsy wood, and within a few days of finding it, small (or large) rodents will be able to nibble through the wood to get inside.

The other problem with ply is the cut surfaces. If they are not sealed to the rain, water will get inside and, during the winter, freeze between the boards. Water, when it freezes actually expands with great force, therefore pushing the boards apart, ruining the wood.

It is preferable to buy hutches made from 'marine ply' or, better still, proper plank wood.

You can get plastic hutches in many designs. There is nothing intrinsically wrong with plastic as a material. Indeed, it does have a number of advantages, and once locked inside, your hens are usually safe from danger. They are usually well ventilated and at the same time free from draughts. Easy to clean, most of them have moulded perches, making it impossible, or at least very difficult, for red mites to gain a hold. However, where the perches are riveted in place, or worse still, made of a pole balanced between holes, it is really difficult to eradicate them.

In a wooden hutch you can blowtorch the mites – but don't burn the thing down! (More on this later.)

Wooden roofs should be at least covered with good-quality roofing felt which should have adequate overhangs and few, or no, seams for water to seep through. Imagine spending the day in the wet, and having to endure the constant dripping rain down your neck all night too!

NESTING BOXES

A rule of thumb is that you should have enough boxes for the birds to be able to use them without having to fight for a space. It's the same problem faced by designers of ladies' toilets. For three birds, have two boxes, for five to seven have three, for eight to ten birds have four and so on. They don't all lay at the same time, but make sure you have lots of space.

Put straw or other materials, such as shredded paper, in the boxes to make them comfortable and reduce the chances of the eggs breaking. I have to confess that the two birds in the plastic hutch have no straw in its single nest box. I first filled it with fresh straw; they ate it. Then I tried them with shredded paper, which they consumed faster than the hay. I then tried fallen soft pine needles, which they ate too. I finally gave up and now the box is bare – and they don't seem to mind. Being plastic, it is moulded to fit a hen smoothly. If I had a box with harsh wooden sides, I would have thought twice, and kept on with the straw.

Some birds can be affected by hay, which I personally I have never experienced, but a kind reader pointed this out to me. The problem is caused by a fungal spore of the *genus aspergillus*. If your birds have a runny nose, it might just be caused by the hay – if you have used it.

Make sure you clean the nesting boxes – hens sometimes poo when they lay, by accident. They sometimes just poo. Actually, that could be the title for the whole book – they do poo quite a lot!

The other thing to remember about nest boxes is fleas and mites. The birds share them, and this is the path to spreading ecto-parasites around the flock, so be sure to regularly clean out the nesting areas, and either disinfect in moderation, dust or otherwise fumigate them regularly.

PROVIDING PERCHES

Hens love to climb up to perch, and they need a branch to hold on to. I remember as a little boy getting chickens' feet from the butcher and frightening girls with them. You pulled on a tendon and the toes clenched. This mechanism is very strong, and once aboard, they never fall off.

So strong is this grip that you from time to time find dead birds still standing on the perch. They need a piece of wood or plastic about an inch to an inch and a half (35 mm) about 50 cm from the ground. You can have another at 75 cm if you are housing more birds.

Try to make sure these perches are smoothly located, with no nooks for red mite to climb into. Once every couple of days look underneath, and where the perch is located into the walls, check for red mite. They huddle together in the shade (they hate light) and look to all intents like a scab. At night, when the birds are roosting, they crawl out of their hiding place on to the birds' legs, and suck their blood. Vampires that they are, they skulk back home in the morning.

Fortunately you don't need a wooden stake to kill them – just some red mite powder.

PROVIDING A LITTER TRAY

While they are up there, having a sleep, hens poo. They poo just as they are going to sleep, when they are asleep and just as they wake up! You will find lines of poo where they have been roosting. Put something down to soak it all up: straw, shredded newspaper, and weekly if possible, collect the lot and compost it. This makes brilliant compost, especially if you are going to grow mushrooms on it, so long as you can get over having a foodstuff created by collecting your hens' poo.

Years ago, although possibly there are one or two still practising it, there was a system called deep littering. You covered the poo with a layer of straw. Each week you piled more straw on it and as it fermented (and ponged a bit too) the litter would fall under its own weight, and warm the hutches in the process.

Then, of course, eventually the deep litter had to be removed, making everyone sweat and sick at the same time.

This is not a good idea for domestic chicken-keeping because of the smell.

PROVIDING A BIG ENOUGH RUN

Most hen hutches come with the possibility of having a run attached to the hut, so the birds get the opportunity for a walk-about, a scratch and a peck and, at the same time, remain protected from the outside world.

For goodness' sake – make it a run!

It is fairly important, and I have often felt this while watching them at the numerous little arks you see in gardens and poultry sales organisations, the word 'run' is a bit of a misnomer, and might in some cases do more harm than good. Maybe I am humanising things too much, but bear with me – you'll get the idea.

In a battery farm the hens look out at row after row of crates, in dimmed but adequate light in a warm, biologically-controlled room.

That's all they see, and they have no notion of anything better or different. But in some cases, in one of those tiny 'arks', they are confined to a space not that much bigger than a battery hen, and the prospect of some wonderful food just out of beak's reach might be far more frustrating to the bird than to be locked up altogether in a warm room with food and water on tap.

If you are going to have a run, make it a run, not a small walk. Remember the five freedoms mean the animal should be able to engage in normal behaviour. We sometimes compare domestic fowl housing with poultry caging, which is not only misleading but possibly unhelpful. If all your birds can do is to waddle around a few square metres of run, that is not enough. In the wild, hens wander many hundreds of metres, to return to their favourite roosts each evening.

If you can, allow the birds the use of the garden space, providing you can protect your favourite flowers, and they cannot get over the fence to decimate your neighbour's garden too.

One of the best runs I have seen was a fruit cage: big enough for a good run, light enough to move, secure enough to keep your birds enclosed.

Make sure the run is predator-proof, and make it so the myriad sparrows and other birds cannot get into the run, or on top of it for that matter. Their droppings could spread disease to your birds.

Do not think the gate to the run is a good enough door for the birds to spend the night behind. Always make sure you can still lock the hut door with the run closed too. and that the run and hut are easily moved by humans, but steady as a rock to wind, children, pets and other animals.

SITING THE HUT

It is best if you can site your hens so they are not overhung by trees, but do have a measure of protection from prevailing winds.

If possible, have a clear gap between the hutch and the ground. This is so there is nowhere for families of rats or mice to live under the hut. Also, if you can construct it so that your hens can climb up to roost, so much the better as it makes them feel more content.

MOVING THE POSITION OF THE HUT AND RUN

As you will have noticed so far in this book, it is alarming how much birds poo. Over time this poo loads the soil it lands on with parasites' spores and eggs which will re-infect your birds, and infect any new birds you may acquire, over time.

One way of reducing the burden of parasites is to move your hens around from time to time. Usually you should put the run and hut on new land every three months, and not return them to the original spot for at least six months.

There are ways of doing this if you just don't have space enough to move them. You can put the birds on concrete or paving flags, covered with a layer of compost or soil both for comfort and to enable them to scratch. This allows you to remove soiled material for composting, along with the parasites in it.

STORING FOOD

This is particularly important if you live in a town. Keep your food away from the hens in a sealable, animal-proof, container. Lock it away in a shed somewhere and always clean up any spillage. It is not good enough to simply store sacks of feed – they are far too easily nibbled through. I used an old steel ammunition chest for many years, and also a set of steel office filing cabinets.

USING A BROODY BOX

From time to time, according to the bird type, your hens will go broody. That is, they'll wish to sit on eggs in order to raise new hens. Such hens become troublesome, pecking at anyone or any hen that comes near the nest box. If you wish the hen to raise a clutch, put some fertile eggs under her and separate her from the main flock. For this you need a broody box, which is essentially a small hutch which allows you to keep the broody and her offspring away from the rest of the hens – who might just kill the young if they could get to them.

The box should have a small but well protected run, free from draughts and rain and there should be a nest box as well as a perch inside. You should be able to feed chick food, and the ability for a mother hen to enjoy a quick walk around, a chance of a poo and have her own food and water.

Alternatively, you may not wish your broody hen to sit on eggs. A few days in the broody box, where there are no eggs to sit on, usually does the trick when it comes to returning her to normality.

BUILDING YOUR OWN CHICKEN HUT

This is a possibility for anyone with the skills. A seriously-robust structure can be made using exterior plywood. A simple box with a door will do.

I built a hen hutch having bought one that came by mail order which arrived smashed to pieces. You need:

- ▶ 1 piece of 18 mm × 60 cm sq exterior ply;
- ▶ 5 pieces of 18mm × 59 cm sq exterior ply;
- ▶ 2 pieces of 3 cm × 1 cm × 60 cm;
- ▶ 2 pieces of 3 cm × 1 cm × 62 cm;
- ▶ lots of nails;
- ▶ a good saw.

What I designed became a hen hutch for 20 quid, that any idiot could put together and that would be at least as good as anyone else's on the market. I have seen similar huts as these for £300 plus and – I know I am biased – but this little hutch is as good as those (I would say that, wouldn't I?).

Making the rooflid

Looking at hen arks, there are hinges, etc., special joints and bits of wood that have to be sawn and even routed. Well, all that fancy stuff is great if you can do it, but I can't, although I can nail a batten to a piece of marine ply, and then use this as a lid.

Having thought about it, the rooflid is a brilliant idea because you can pull it off and reach into the hutch to clean it. The roosting bar can be lifted out and all the nooks and crannies can be got at with a blow lamp to remove all the red mites, or dusted or cleaned.

The volume inside is very similar to my Omlet Eglu – plenty of space for two birds, and lots of headroom for the birds to breathe the fresh air.

To start with you need four pieces of 18 mm marine ply 59 cm square and one 60 cm square. You need another piece of ply which you will fit in the front. I didn't bother to measure this piece, I just marked this off.

You need some 3 cm × 1 cm batten with which to line the outer edge of the 60 cm square lid. This will give you a lid with a lip, which you can lay on top of the box.

When the hut is finished you have a choice – you can either put roofing felt on the rooflid or paint it. I had some rubberised paint in the shed, and I quite fancied that.

The rooflid will be fixed in place with a bungee (nylon-cased elasticated band) so it can't blow away. My first design idea was to have a dowel through two holes on which the bungee could lip over and the birds could roost on it. But I now prefer a fixed roost.

Siting the roosting bar
Mark out the position of the roosting bar before you put the whole hut together. This must be at least 20 cm from the back wall, and a minimum of 15 cm off the floor, preferably higher if you can manage it. There should be headroom of at least 30 cm.

Clamping and construction
The sides of the hutch sit on top of the floor piece and are screwed and glued into position. I found it easier to hold the pieces in position with clamps. Actually constructing your hut is a little fiddly to set up, but when using clamps, the whole job is much easier to complete.

Fixing the back
The floor is fixed to the two side walls and the whole structure is then strengthened by attaching the back. The structure now has a floor and three sides, glued and screwed together.

The front

Cut a piece, about 3 sq cm, out of the top of the front, to allow for ventilation.

The entrance (door) is also cut out of the front piece and can be hinged, slid behind two L-shaped brackets, or held in position with rope. The size of the entrance is really the most important part of the construction, because this is where Mr Fox could get in. If you make the entry space just big enough for a hen to get through, you will make your hut safer against predators. However, if you make the aperture too small, the hens will not use it, leaving themselves vulnerable to attack.

Nest box and roost bar in place

First, cover the structure completely with roofing felt, for waterproofing. The whole structure needs either to be painted or treated with wood preservative.

Your hut must be raised off the ground. You could construct a wooden frame for this purpose, but you might just as well use some concrete blocks.

The cost

Already-treated marine ply costs around 30 a sheet, which provides more than enough to make a small hut. You will have to maintain for your hut, by keeping it painted and weatherproofed, but these tips prove that keeping hens doesn't have to be expensive.

INTRODUCING HENS TO THEIR NEW HOME

This is a tricky affair if you already have hens. Let us assume first of all that you have none, and these are your first birds.

Some people put their hens on the perch so they can feel at home. I never do this for two reasons. First of all, and this is especially true if you have got yourself some ex-battery hens: you don't know how strong the grip is and they can fall off and hurt themselves. When you buy birds they can be from a holding pen where they have spent their previous couple of weeks.

Of course, ex-battery hens are fragile creatures to start with, and should never be offered a perch to stand on if they are not willing to do so.

Place the birds in their hut with food and water and confine them for 24 hours, long enough for them to become content with their new surroundings. Then let them into the run and only after a week or two let them wander into the garden at large.

INTRODUCING HENS TO EACH OTHER

If your hens have been raised from chicks – which is quite likely if you buy them from a dedicated poultry supplier – they will have formed bonds of 'friendships' that mean they more or less live peacefully for most of their lives together.

Cockerels, from a fairly young age, are competitive. They don't ever stop being so. They will fight with increasing ferociousness to gain as many females in their harem as possible. Bringing a new bird into an established flock can be fraught with problems because that bonding is not there between the established birds and the newcomer and they will, likely as not, encounter some problems, ranging from a bit of bok-boking to outright bullying.

If possible, introduce at least two new birds at the same, time, putting them in a broody box next to the fence and give them their own little run. Watch out for skirmishes at the fence between the established and new birds. You will know if there is a problem if there is a heightened amount of bok-bok-boking going on.

Only when you feel happy should you put them into the same run, when you must watch their behaviour carefully. It can take a week for these two sets of hens to be united, and even then, a firm eye needs to be kept open for trouble.

CHAPTER 7

HOW TO KEEP YOUR HENS HEALTHY AND CLEAN

Hens are fairly clean in their habits. I say fairly clean meaning that they will preen themselves, oil their feathers and make sure these are waterproof. However, they will poo in their food and water, where they sleep, and will eat spilled feed lodged in poo and mud if they're hungry enough.

Like all birds who are mobile enough in the wild to avoid having special behaviour when it comes to excreting, hens do not mind soiling themselves. Pigs, on the other hand, are completely fastidious about not pooing on themselves; not so hens!

Consequently, we have to keep our birds clean. This means cleaning out from the hutch their roosting messes, and making sure any places where hens stand or sit are free from both mess and ectoparasites.

CLEANING THE HUTCH

It is often better if cleaning can be managed every couple of days, a task easier if you only have a few birds to clean up after. My advice would be to start composting chicken manure as early as possible. A decent compost heap would soon be overloaded by the amount of manure produced by chickens, and the compost would become runny and smelly.

The important thing is to be sure to add a lot of garden waste and mix this with layers of chicken manure. A good compost heap needs heat, air and water to work well. If you keep on removing the lid in order to add a small amount of hen manure in the heap, it will soon cool down, thus reducing its efficiency. Collect a week's worth in a lidded bucket and then add this to the heap. First put in a few sheets of newspaper and then add the manure, then more newspaper on top. By doing this you will have plenty of absorbent newspaper and the heap will remain healthy.

DON'T OVER-DISINFECT

The temptation to make the hen hutch completely sterile like our own toilets should be avoided. If any staining or smearing of poo occurs, wash it away with a little salted water. Try to avoid strong vapours which the birds dislike and which can taint eggs.

If you can remove the majority of the manure using newspaper, a brush, a draw hoe or a shovel, that is all you really need to do. I find a watering can works to wash away the rest of the debris with a quick brushing.

I sprinkle some salt to disinfect and then re-bed the floor with whatever material I am using at the time.

A serious look around the perch(es), the joints and nooks and crannies inside the hutch will show up red mites, which should be removed and treated/eliminated, and you should be looking for telltale signs of rodents getting into the hut – spraints (rodent faeces) are quite different from chicken poo. If you find any, establish where they are getting into the hut and deal with this accordingly. I have found that sealing the hole and raising the hut from the ground (if that is possible) deals with the little visitors.

CLEANING THE NEST BOXES

I tend to do this between every few days and a week. However, if the nest box is soiled, I clean it straight away. It is a matter of cleaning away the bedding material and replacing it, looking out for mites, etc. and dealing with them accordingly, and making sure you are constantly happy with the quality of the eggs. We will look at this later, but they can sometimes be streaked with poo or blood or both, which sometimes also gets on the bedding. This could indicate a poorly hen.

If you have a lot of poo in the nest box, this could mean you have a hen with a bowel/reproducitve passage problem, a hen sleeping on the nest box, or a lazy hen. Watch your birds for signs of bullying if you have a hen roosting on the side of the nest box. If possible, take the box away for a night and listen at roosting time for signs of trouble.

CLEANING FEEDERS

This is an important task. Hens will soil their water, given the chance, and so you have to clean it. Always make sure the drinking pans are clean – no algae in them and certainly no poo! You wouldn't wish to drink from them and neither do the hens. You might wonder why they poo around the drinking vessels – they can't help it. They have evolved a lifestyle on the move, over a great area, but we keep them like agricultural beasts, confined, so their natural behaviour doesn't match how we keep them.

Make sure you also clean the feeder, whether hopper or dish. Keep it dry and don't let food spill out too much (although this can't be helped, believe me!).

CHAPTER 8

CHOOSING YOUR BIRDS

It has been my experience that, like bees, hens are fascinating. They will absorb your sleepless nights and provide you with no end of interest. There is always something new to learn, always something to prepare for or look forward to.

There is no such thing as the best hen, the right hen, the one you should buy, because there are so many factors involved in their care and use. You might fancy something that looks pretty around the garden, you might want a large meat variety, a good layer or a combination of all three. You might fancy bantams, which are small versions of the ordinary breeds or you might prefer to do your bit for henkind and keep ex-battery birds.

The whole thing is up to you, you're the boss. But there are some breeds that do better for the garden poultry keeper than others.

WHAT ARE THE ADVANTAVES OF KEEPING A COCKEREL?

We have said, on page 18, that in the town, where there are neighbours to annoy, you are best not to keep a cockerel. But, and I am not contradicting myself at all, there are good reasons for keeping one. Of course, the overriding concern should be the people around you. But, generally speaking, hens are happier with cockerels. Of course, their natural passion is to reproduce, one of the defining qualities of life itself, and the presence of the cockerel keeps hens in order, and fulfills this urge for them.

With a cockerel in your flock the hens will also be protected to a degree.

Cockerels are fussy, bloody-minded and strong, and many a cat or dog has been put off by their presence. There has been lots of research into the importance of hen society, and the way they perceive threats, and it has been found that they are definitely happier with a man around.

HOW TO BUY HENS

Always keep more than one

Chickens are flocking birds, albeit in reduced numbers than many breeds, but they are social animals. A lone hen is a sad beast indeed and I would say the minimum number of birds to start with is three – just in case one dies there are still two to be going on with. It is not uncommon for single hens to give up the will to live, and they are enlivened when put with another hen.

Ex-battery

There are lots of ways of getting hens. Perhaps one of the safest, with regard to the health of the birds and their future development, is to buy ex-battery hens from one of the organisations such as the British Hen Welfare Trust.

I agree, in the long run, with many who say these birds might not be the best birds for a brand new hen enthusiast. There are instances where a bird can die of shock, cold, stress and new hen keepers are apt to blame themselves in these situations. It isn't the best introduction to keeping poultry to have one die. But generally ex-battery hens are very healthy indeed. They might look featherless and bewildered, but this is partly because of the moult – which is why they are no use to the egg farmer in the first place.

The point is that an ex-battery hen has been immunised against almost everything treatable in the hen world, they have no lice or mites, their guts are clear of parasites and so on.

You should give them land that has not had hens on it before – if they ingest worms or parasites they can become quite ill because they haven't had them before. They need plenty of shelter, good food and clean water and time to recover from their entry into the world – a bit of peace and quiet.

You can buy special ex-battery feed with a little extra protein to help them recover their feathers, and then as soon as they start laying again put them on layers' pellets.

Ex-battery hens are hybrids, built for egg laying. You will get at least 250 eggs from each bird in the next year – their previous year they probably laid around 340 eggs.

Buying from producers

I would say, don't buy from an agricultural market by auction. It is a waste of time because you have absolutely no idea what you are buying, the state of the birds, their age and what not. There are, however, a number of poultry shows around the country where specialist producers sell their stock.

I know this sounds obvious, but do make sure you have all the housing, feed, waterers, everything you need, in place before you buy and you have adequate boxes for the birds to be transported home.

At dedicated poultry shows you can talk to suppliers, ask questions, compare birds and pick up a lot of advice on the way that you might never get elsewhere.

Poultry parks

These include poultry 'farms' where you can go and view the hens, often rare breed hens at that, poultry housing, poultry feed and even get training. Very often they are very good, but look around at the cleanliness of the huts and runs and the way the birds interact. Are the waterers clean and so on?

Don't forget to ask questions such as, 'What are the hens immunised against?',

'Can you show me they are at point of lay?' – a question that often brings many answers.

Shop around and visit a few – they're nice days out anyway.

Pol

This means point of lay, in other words these hens are just about ready to start laying eggs. You will find many poultry sellers will call a bird POL at 18 weeks, and you could be waiting another six before they actually start to lay – a maddening period when you actually hardly believe it is ever going to happen.

Be patient – feed them good food and eventually they will start.

You can get an indication about POL if, when handling the bird, you can fit two fingers between the pelvic bones near the hen's bottom. This gap increases in size the nearer the animal is to laying.

BREEDS SUITABLE FOR EVERYONE

Pure breeds vs hybrids

Over the years people have bred poultry to get certain characteristics, crossing a good layer with a bird that never moults to give something of both characteristics. However, usually, these birds when mated produce all kinds of offspring none of them resembling their parents.

Over many generations, people have produced some birds that always breed true – they are called pure breeds.

The ancona, for example, produces anconas, not a larger male without barrs and a smaller female almost black.

Hybrid birds are not like this. If you mate two hybrids you are most likely not to get anything because many of them are sterile, or some of them don't produce males at all. Sometimes hybrids produce some very strange offspring, as the genetics of their grandparents show through.

Sex linkage

There are characteristics that are linked to the sex of the bird. For most of us this is of little importance until we start to breed our hens. Sometimes, for example, males can have telltale markings, allowing us to separate them from the rest of the chicks – unless you are willing to grow them for food, no one wants a lot of cockerels!

The following birds are ones of which I have had some personal experience and can vouch for their characteristics. There are many more birds out there to choose from – around 160 pure breeds alone, so go and have a look! They are always fascinating, and a closer study will bring enjoyment and reward.

The LBJ to Mrs Pepperpot

These are hybrid birds that are so widespread they are often referred to as Little Brown Jobbies or LBJs. They are mostly from the breeding programmes that have produced the ubiquitous battery hen.

There are a number of reasons for keeping these hens, in addition to their heavy egg-laying capabilities. They are patient, unruffled birds that are gentle and very bonding. Once they know you they will come and eat from your hand. They are perfect for children and rarely fight or bully.

Robust, they can withstand freezing temperatures and summer heat, and are very economical birds.

One of the great things about them is they hardly ever go broody, a trait bred out of them.

You can find these birds anywhere, and their characteristics are fairly common.

Most of the LBJs you buy are crosses with Rhode Island Red (RIR). Miss Pepperpot, for example, is a cross between an RIR and another hybrid cross between a Maran and a Plymouth Rock. The Speckledy Hen is a cross between an RIR and a Maran.

Ancona

These are compact birds, almost halfway between full-sized birds and bantams. They have been around since the 1840s and produce in the region of 170 smallish eggs a year. They are prone to fighting, and though they are striking in appearance, you have to be careful – they do not mix well with children. However, if you are looking for a bird that will wander around the allotment, vacuuming up insects, this is the one for you.

Australorp

A dual-purpose bird developed for the outbackers in Australia. It lays around 200 eggs a year and has a decent carcass too. This bird does tend to broodiness, and they do make excellent mothers, so if you are thinking about breeding, this is the one for you – the broody process is usually pain free.

You will notice that hens with black feathers lay fewer eggs than average, whereas birds with red/brown feathers lay more. The Australorp is just about the exception that proves the rule. Just imagine what would have been the case if these birds were RIR-based!

Barnevelder

This is a beautifully dappled bird you just want to hug (but don't). It is a docile, friendly bird that will hoover up insects and garden pests and still find time for a chat in the middle of the day. It has to be one of the best birds for the garden – not too big and easy to care for. The downside is the lowish number of eggs, at around 170.

Black Rock

This is a hybrid of the RIR and the Barred Plymouth Rock. They look gorgeous, being black with some chestnut. They are lovely birds to be near, and they are gentle with each other and other hens.

If you live in the north of the UK, or in an exposed, cold windy place, the Black Rock is the bird for you. It has strong, highly waterproofed feathers that keep the bird dry and warm in the worst of weathers.

Their feathers are very strong and they are prolific layers – around 230 a year. They are well worth a look if you want a possibly more handsome version of the LBJ.

Orpington

These are a little like pillows on legs. They are nearly all feather, and consequently striking birds. These are the most docile birds in the world, and love being picked up. They are easy with pets and children. They are so mild that they do not react well when there are other bossy birds around – watch out for feather pecking.

They only lay around 150 eggs a year, but are seriously buff and lovely.

Plymouth Rock

This is an American bird of long pedigree, hailing back to the 1820s. I have only really kept white ones, but you can also get buff-coloured examples. It is not a small bird, making a good boiler, but still laying about 160 eggs a year. This is an example of the dual-purpose bird, producing meat and eggs, and is therefore the smallholder's ideal hen.

If you keep them penned into a small run, they will grow fat quite quickly, but allow them the garden to roam around and they walk it off. Extremely docile, this animal is a great companion.

Rhode Island Red

There is something masterful about these birds. They stand no nonsense in the run, but are not outrageously aggressive. It's just the way they stand! They look like members of the hen SAS, but lay lots of eggs – around 220 a year.

They need space and are big birds, so choose your housing carefully.

Sussex

These are lovely birds to keep – if you like white hens with all kinds of little markings and beautiful temperaments. These birds are inquisitive – always on the go, looking for something to do, scratching and intelligent. They are not too large, lay around 200 eggs a year and have soft feathers – so keep them sheltered from driving rain.

Wyandottes

These pure breed birds are such gentle barred and speckled hens. I had a number of them, silver laced, and they were just lovely. Almost too lovely – I was always worried they would break a bone. With slight frames but quite robust really, they lay about 200 eggs a year.

Bantams

The bonsai of the chicken world, bantams are miniature versions of the larger breeds – mostly pure breed chickens. They are a delight to keep because they seem (to me at least) to have bags of personality.

Generally they tend to have the same characteristics, especially with regard to egg laying, as their larger counterparts. However, do not think that, because they are small, you need less space.

Some poultry books describe bantams as being 'flighty'. They can be aggressive, and certainly are much more mobile than the larger birds. They fly more easily and generally need a lot of room for their size.

They eat a similar amount of food to a larger bird, but give smaller eggs. It has to be said, the eggs are gorgeous! They are thicker shelled and have just as much nutritional value in them as larger eggs, and are excellent fried and boiled. In cakes, you just need to use more of them.

They tend to do well when mixed with larger birds, and it is better if there are three or four of them together. They tend to hold their own and are rarely bothered by bullying hens – partly because they are faster, and partly because they give as good as they get.

CHAPTER 9

HOW TO RECOGNISE WHEN THINGS ARE GOING WRONG

Designwise, hens are simple. There is not a lot that can go wrong with them, but when it does, they do down quickly. They have a habit of giving up when they are really poorly and they are easy to spot when they do.

The main thing about hens is they have a signal on the top of their head telling you how they are doing. Often the first sign of a bird being off colour is a droopy, pale comb. We do not intend to list all the diseases your birds can get, nor all the remedies.

One of the best things you can do is find a vet who has hen experience, just in case, and then maintain a good feeding, watering and cleaning regime. This is the key to success with hens: good food, clean water, lack of stress and plenty of fresh air.

APPLE CIDER VINEGAR (ACV)

This brilliant substance aids poultry's immune system so much that it promotes health. You really can see a difference when you add it to the hens' water. They perk up and actually look happy. It works both as an antiseptic and an antibiotic; it reduces parasite load in the gut and promotes healing.

All you need to do is add two dessert spoons per litre to their drinking water. Do this every day for a week each month.

OTHER ADDITIVES

There are many companies selling tonics for hens, often containing garlic and other vitamins. Usually they deal with internal parasites and are of some use in this respect. They are not to be used instead of a wormer because they will not remove nor kill all the worms in the hen. They will just help to keep them down.

Garlic is also an antibiotic, always beneficial in keeping hens healthy.

HENS SITTING IN THE CORNER, HARDLY FEEDING OR DRINKING

This is a typical bullying situation. Hens are not like us – they bully and there is a 'pecking order'. Females will often gang up on a weaker bird, pecking at her until blood is drawn. When they taste blood, hens are encouraged to carry on doing what they are doing, making it worse for the victim. Bullied hens sleep on nest boxes, hardly ever get to their food, or water. They sit, listless, in a corner of the run and look scruffy.

The way to deal with this problem is to remove the hen from the others into a little run and hutch of her own. She will quickly pick up after her ordeal; a few good sleeps, and feeding and watering will set her right. She might never be able to rejoin the flock, though.

You might find there is one hen, or maybe a cock, who is causing all the trouble, and isolating that bird can often put things right. It is a question of watching your hens, knowing what they are doing and acting accordingly.

HENS WITH FEATHERS MISSING

From time to time hens pluck feathers, and there is nothing wrong with that. However, this can sometimes be due to a couple of problems that need treating. When hens pull feathers from around their bottoms, often with enough force to cause bleeding, it can be due to the irritation of chicken mites.

You can buy powder for the birds, and treatment for the hut. You have to remove the birds from the hut also all the bedding and clean away any poo. Make sure all the inside of the hut is treated with the powder, and dust the birds too.

You might wish to keep the affected birds in isolation until they have healed in order to avoid pecking. Be sure you treat all your birds.

Sometimes feather pulling can be a reaction to stress, especially if there are too many birds in a small space. The remedy here is to make more room available, or remove some birds.

WHITE ENCRUSTING AT THE BASE OF THE FEATHERS

This is the debris and the eggs of the chicken louse. It really irritates the birds, leading to feather pulling. Clean out the hut and apply louse powder to the nest boxes, etc. and treat the birds.

BIRDS WITH SCALY LEGS

Hens' legs should be perfectly smooth, but they can sometimes become encrusted and painful. This is a problem caused by mites that get under the scales of the leg where they lay eggs and generally irritate the bird. In bad cases the bird can have difficulty in walking.

You can rub oil on the legs which will suffocate the mites underneath. A vet treatment also does the same thing, but more effectively. If your hens get scaly leg it is probably best to seek advice.

LOTS OF DIARRHOEA AND HUNGRY BIRDS

When egg production drops and there is a lot of diarrhoea it may mean that your hens have worms. They need to be wormed at least twice a year. Worming powder is sprinkled on their food and this does the trick. Moving the hens to fresh pasture also helps reduce or prevent re-infection.

PALE COMBS AND REDUCED EGG PRODUCTION

This could be due to almost anything, but the first check should be for red mite. These pests spend the day hiding in crevices and their nights drinking the blood of your birds. Bad cases will leave your birds anaemic and with scaly leg problems.

Check for red mite at least every week and kill them. There are lots of ways of killing them, from powders to sprays to diatomaceous earth to blow torches. Check all the crannies in the hutch, and don't forget the nest boxes too.

WHEEZING BIRDS

This can be due to a number of problems, but perhaps the most common is aspergillosis, a fungus that infests hay and poo in the hut and whose spores are breathed in by the hens. This can irritate the lining of the hens' lungs. The aspergillum fungus can also live inside the bird. There is no cure for this, but your birds can be kept going with good feed, clean huts and plenty of fresh air and clean water.

CHAPTER 10

WHAT MAKES A CHICKEN TICK?

We once had a ticking chicken. It ticked for about a day and my grandfather thought he had lost his watch. It was too loud a tick for his old hunter anyway, and I later wondered if the chicken had eaten some largish pebbles, and on moving its muscular sack, called the gizzard, the ticking occurred. I have never heard another hen tick.

The insides of the hen are fairly simple, and you don't need to know the hen's anatomy in order to keep them, but a little knowledge, apart from being a dangerous thing, always enhances one's enjoyment.

THE CHICKEN GUT AND HOW IT WORKS

Everyone knows that hens do not have teeth. They have a marked drive to peck at anything that looks like a crumb. The chicken's digestive system is wonderfully adapted to allow the bird to get the most out of a little food. The advantage of being able to fly has meant that the chicken's digestive system has to be lightweight. Hens really are more efficient digesters than most other animals.

Food is swallowed and makes its way to the crop where it can be stored for some time. If you handle your birds you can feel the crop, often full of food, which passes to the proventriculus and the gizzard.

In the proventriculus enzymes are added to the food, starting the process of digestion, and fairly quickly the food is passed on to the gizzard. Here stones enable the grinding of the enzyme-enriched food from the proventriculus. There are hard, horny ridges in the wall of the gizzard and plenty of efficient muscle to churn the mass inside.

From here food is passed into the small intestine, where the nutrients are absorbed. The small intestine is a long, coiled tube containing many blood vessels. The remainder of the undigested material passes into the large intestine and from there into the cloaca, which is a complex chamber essentially made up of three flaps in a void. One of the flaps comes from the common egg laying and urine pathways, the second from the gut itself, and the final opening into the vent itself.

The undigested food is mixed with urine in the cloaca and comes out as poo – lots of it! A good chicken poo is solidish (soft to touch, but don't bother) with a white blob on the top. This consists of uric acid crystals – the urine part.

Adjoining the intestine, are two long sacs called the caeca. These are not unlike the appendix, and hold digesting material. Sometimes long fluffy masses of poo are produced when the hens empty the caeca.

The liver, like all such organs, is involved in changing the chemicals absorbed from the digestive system to others needed by the chicken for its life and growth. And, of course, it makes brilliant paté!

HOW HENS MAKE EGGS

This is quite an important topic because there is much to be learned about the hen by the state of her eggs. Also you get an insight into the cycles of the hen.

Hens have a string of eggs which they lay is sequence, approximately two eggs every three days. Sometimes there are more than this, other times less. Once the egg has left the ovary it undergoes a number of changes, on its passage towards the outside world.

The membranes are laid over the yolk, and filled out, and finally the calcareous shell is laid on top, producing the egg as we know it. Your hens need a good supply of calcium in their diet, otherwise the shells will become progressively thinner.

As the egg reaches the end of its duct, the sheer size pushes closed the large intestine and it exits via the cloaca.

Conversely, when the hen is removing waste the mass of faeces pushes closed the egg-bearing duct, stopping backwards movement of the material into the egg-laying organs and passage.

Hens are stimulated to produce eggs by sunlight, and therefore you get fewer eggs in winter than in summer. Some poultry keepers use artificial light in the hutch to keep the egg production to a maximum, but I personally have never tried this.

Hens have a finite number of eggs in a particular string. Their first year is their most productive and a good layer will have about 300 eggs. Their egg yield decreases year on year. When a particular string is used up, the hens go into the moult before starting to lay again. The moult is a food holiday, a chance for the hen to rejuvenate herself before having again to undertake the arduous task of producing and laying so many eggs. It is often a time when a hen will go broody.

THE MOULT

This is characterised by the loss of feathers, lack of comb colour, generally scruffy appearance and no eggs. The bird is, however, eating well, and within a few weeks she looks fine. Having clipped the hen's wing when she was a youngster, you will have to do it again after the moult because her flight feathers will have been replaced.

There is nothing you can do to speed the moult, and neither should you. The hens have earned this period of R&R.

BROODINESS

Because of a genetic propensity, some breeds go broody at the drop of a hat, others never do so. You can decide to let a hen sit on a clutch of fertile eggs – assuming you have a cockerel. Hens store sperm, but get a regular supply in some cases every few hours, so you can be sure that laying hens in the presence of a cockerel produce fertile eggs.

You can recognise a broody hen. She goes flat, sits on eggs and won't move – pecking the hand that tries to move her. I try to remove the broody hen, nest box and eggs, to a broody box and run at this point, giving her peace and the rest of the hens a chance to get near the nest boxes without being molested.

The hen will take 21 days to incubate her clutch. Hens have the amazing ability to allow the eggs to chill for a short while and they will not start to develop until the mother hen warms them up – thus timing the chicks' arrivals all at the same time – more or less.

When the chicks start to hatch she will take a couple of days to leave the unhatched eggs, and then will continue the task of looking after her chicks.

The chicks need a warm and dry place to grow. Most of the time the broody hen will continue with her task of being a good mother, but sometimes she simply decides otherwise. If she is not letting the chicks under her to keep warm, they need to be removed to an area with a lamp for warmth.

CRUMBS

The chicks need chick crumbs to eat, and the mother hen will eat them too. If you add some hard-boiled egg, all the better. They also need plenty of fresh water to drink supplied in such a way that they cannot fall over and drown in it. I have used a dish with pebbles in it, but special drinkers are also available which keep the chicks' downy feathers dry – an important matter if they get cold. Both the drinker and the feeder will be messed in by the chicks, and even by the mother hen. You should clean it every time you see it dirty – many times a day!

When the chicks are about a week old, add some chick grit so they can get their gizzards working properly. Keep an eye on the chicks – they get themselves into trouble, falling over stuff, getting stuck in netting and the edges of the broody hutch.

When they are about six weeks old, feed them growers' pellets, a richer formula with extra protein, which I keep them on until point of lay.

WHAT ARE YOU GOING TO DO ABOUT COCKERELS?

First, chicks die. Despite everything we do for them, they die. You need not to beat yourself up about it, learn where necessary, and make sure you are up to the task of disposing of the chicks at the earliest opportunity.

More importantly, you will get 50% cockerels, possibly more than 50%! With mortality at around 20%, from a clutch of a dozen chicks you might lose a few, and only have three females.

You need to be able to deal with the males. It really isn't fair to keep them, and it is best to decide from the outset what you will do with them all.

CARING FOR YOUR HENS AROUND THE YEAR

Winter and spring
Your hens will need careful attention in the wet, short days of winter. Expect to feed them more and get less eggs. The day's length gives messages to the hen's reproductive system, telling it there is no point in laying because any chicks will not be viable.

Handle your birds early on
It is a good idea to handle your birds so you get to know how their bodies are

working. A plump fleshy bird is obviously doing well; a bird with its bones sticking out is doing less well. In late autumn assess the birds – how they are doing, and if there are any needing extra care.

Give them all a dose of Apple Cider Vinegar and worm them.

Cut down their ongoing garden activities and move the run to the most sheltered part of the garden or provide shelter for them. Protect them from the rain – driving rain kills weak hens.

Clean the huts and use good bedding and, as much as possible, confine the birds to their run, which I fill with compost and clean out regularly. I also have a number of paving slabs along the run; this is to avoid them getting muddy. Mud can be quite harmful to the birds. It clogs their feet, saps their energy by being cold and can be full of microbes not beneficial to hens.

Give hens extra feed. This can take the form of vegetables – if they are penned up they get bored, so this is a psychological treat as well as a health benefit. In freezing weather give them some corn at night, and put glycerine in the water to stop it becoming hard.

If you notice your hens wheezing, make sure this is treated before the winter, as problems can quickly spread around the flock. If you can, house hens prone to bullying separately. This is because they can cause havoc in a crowded run or hut.

Hens are good at withstanding cold, not so good with wet and cold. If it is driving rain and sleet, high winds and so on leave them indoors if you can. One of the best places is a polytunnel – where they scratch around the empty beds and poo on the compost. Don't forget, however, to bring them in!

As the days lengthen you will find your birds come to life. They enjoy the light that spring brings and are seriously happy to be in it.

Move the run off the winter land and give them some scratching space. Check for lice and red mite etc., and they will be happy to reward you with increased egg production.

Summer and autumn

Remember an important fact: sunlight makes for luxuriant growth. As the plants grow, so do the animals that live off plants. Your hens will be chomping on weeds and all kinds of plant growth. As the hens grow, so do the animals that live off the hens. There are more threats, hungry vixens with even hungrier young and hungry badgers ready to demolish your military style defences to get to your hens. So be vigilant!

That said, it is not just the big animals that increase in number – just like the varroa mite in the bee hive, mice, rats, mites, lice and any number of parasites are on the increase too.

Summertime is a time of worming, delousing, removing red mite and general health control. Check particularly the bottom for mites – whiteness and egg cases, the hens' ears for mites (you don't always think of hens having ears but they do, behind some feathers on either side of the head, below the eyes).

Provide shade and dusty areas for the birds to wallow in and plenty of fresh food once they have taken their daily amount of pellets.

Hens can get sunstroke in really hot weather. If shade isn't enough and you have a panting, collapsing bird, the books say to plunge it in cold (not freezing) water for a few seconds. I have only had to do this once, in a bucket. I held her firmly and just dunked her except her head, in a bucket of water. She looked shocked at first, but then completely recovered.

PART TWO
DUCKS

CHAPTER 11

INTRODUCTION TO DUCKS

I had a friend, well, he seemed like a friend, though I never met him. I did write a book about him, and pretty much inherited the use of all of his papers, his films, his music and, of course, his pipes. Jack Hargreaves was an interesting man. He was editor of *Picture Post* in the 1950s and in his office – maybe it was a joke – he built a gun punt. With it, he would sneak up on a flock of unsuspecting ducks and shoot them with the huge gun. The gun was so large that it would propel the boat backwards at an alarming rate, and he would then paddle off to collect his quarry.

The reason for my mentioning this is to point out the difference between the people who ate duck and the people who ate chicken, traditionally, in the UK.

This might seem overtly working class, but it is a general truism that since duck was largely seen as game, ordinary people didn't keep them. It is only comparatively recently that people have begun enjoying duck meat. The likes of Jack Hargreaves and his television executive comrades thought nothing of eating duck while the rest of us stuck to chicken.

However, there are many excellent reasons for keeping ducks in the garden, not least that they lay eggs and taste supreme.

GOOD GARDENERS

Ducks will not scratch up your flower and vegetable beds in the way a chicken will. Sure, they waddle around, and they poo quite a lot, but they don't scrabble in the dirt for worms and insects.

They do, however, eat a lot of slugs, and they will keep the population down. (By the way, this is a good reason for the correct cooking of ducks allowed to roam freely around the garden. Slugs carry parasites that can infect humans, and undercooked duck meat can be a way of passing them on. Make sure, if you are going to kill and eat your ducks, that they are properly cooked.)

WHAT YOU NEED TO KEEP DUCKS

Everything said about chicken keeping applies to ducks also, unless specifically mentioned in this section. Ducks, like hens, must be allowed to wander, and you should move them to fresh grass regularly to keep their parasite load down. They need worming too.

Ducks are, along with other breeds of birds, called waterfowl. This means their world is water. They love it, are happiest when in it, and will always profit from it. A pond is an ideal situation for ducks, especially if you can keep it clean. A river, however, might find your ducks five miles away in an hour, unless you can fence it off downstream successfully.

The important thing about water is the ducks need to regularly wash their faces. Their eyes in particular get sticky and need washing. Even if you cannot provide enough space for a pond, you can still keep ducks. I have used an old baby bath (the bath was old, not the baby!) sunk into the garden and filled with water. Of course, please do be careful if you have young children and keep them away from the water.

Ducks don't jump, they waddle, so they cannot handle steps very well. They will rarely bother your raised beds because of this. They are happy to flip-flop their way around the garden.

HOUSING YOUR DUCKS

Housing can be very simple. Ducks will happily live with hens, though it is important they are kept from having hens' droppings fall on them. You need a wider door if you keep ducks – they race for the exit, and since they waddle, they can hurt themselves.

They also need a ramp, because they cannot manage steps or ladders.

Like hens, they need a nest box arrangement so they can lay, which they do in the morning, before 9 a.m. (ish). I don't let them out until after this so they don't lay all over the garden.

If you want to confine them to a run, then this is possible. Captive ducks rarely fly, and a fence about four feet high – just over a metre – is adequate.

The house should be roomy and well-ventilated, and have especially good access for clearing away bedding and poo. Duck poo is wetter and smellier than hen poo, and could do with being cleaned more regularly.

FEEDING YOUR DUCKS

Ducks can find certain hoppers difficult to eat from and I have tended to use an open feeder. However, they do make a mess with their food. It is important to keep your water away from the feed, too – ducks do not like wet food at all.

Ducks will eat chicken pellets. Indeed they will clean up all the pellets chickens leave around in their untidy eating. It is much better, however, to buy specific duck feed. You can also buy duck pellets, specially formulated particularly for growing meat breeds or laying birds.

Like chicken pellets duck feed comes in different regimes and textures, from crumbs for ducklings to mash and pellets for adult birds. You can even buy special floating food, but there isn't really much use for this except for attracting the ducks when you need them.

Although ducks do eat bread, it is not particularly good for them, and you should stick to ordinary feeding and allow the ducks to forage for their extras.

Foraging is an important part of the ducks' lifestyle. They spend their days hoovering the garden for food, and this should not be denied them.

USING YOUR DUCKS FOR MEAT AND EGGS

Clearly, one of the reasons for keeping ducks is for their meat. This is a hard choice, and should be an experienced one. Killing a duck is not easy, for two reasons. First, they are physically difficult to kill by neck dislocation, one of the methods allowed for one-off dispatching. The other method, by a free bullet in the field, is not the easiest thing to arrange, and impossible for the ordinary town garden duck enthusiast.

The other reason why it is difficult is because ducks are so cute, endearing, funny and all round good eggs (forgive the pun). Ducks are fun and you will become as attached to them as your dog or cat – it takes a special kind of person to be able to kill a duck and eat it.

It is physically hard to kill a duck, and you need to be shown rather than be taught by a book. Consequently this part of duck care will not appear here. I say 'duck care' because, as with chickens, ducks sometimes get sick and it is both a responsibility and a kindness to be able to put them out of their misery.

Duck eggs are wonderful. Usually larger and tastier than hen eggs, many breeds produce almost as many eggs as a hen, which is remarkable when you see the size, and they are full of flavour.

Duck egg shells are more porous than chick eggs, and therefore it is best to collect them as soon as possible after laying.

HANDLING DUCKS

This isn't as easy as handling hens. Ducks will be all over the place, running, scattering, calling and making a fuss. They don't come to you as easily as some chickens will and, consequently, you can increase their stress as well as yours by chasing them about. It is much easier to pen them closely together and then take the birds one by one for inspection. This way they cannot move about so easily and if you are firm, confident but kind, you will have no problems. A duck's peck is rather funny, nothing as severe as a stonking kiss from a cockerel, which will draw blood.

DUCK LIFE

Drakes and ducks are often attached, singly or in small groups – somewhat like hens, but with a greater degree of attachment. One of the problems is the drakes are too randy. They will force females into mating several times a day, and if you are not careful ducks can become quite damaged.

There is a pecking order among ducks and the weakest ones get very shoddy treatment from the drakes indeed, so much so that they are frequently damaged. It is a good idea to have some kind of quarantine for hard-done-by ducks.

CHAPTER 12

FEEDING YOUR DUCKS

Ducks are browsers, in that they love to eat from a range of sources. Everyone knows ducks dabble. They up-end in the pond and loosen insects from under stones. They love to eat slugs and snails and will eat vegetable matter too.

However, the garden duck does not have enough room to get its diet in this way. True, there will be extras for them – important extras at that, both nutritionally and socially. But it has to be said that ducks get their feed from us, and it is our responsibility to ensure they have a good diet.

Modern ducks have been bred to be ready for table in as little as two months. They are not, however, able to do this by foraging for their own dinner. It is important to realize these animals have been bred (call it genetic engineering by old-fashioned methods if you like) to be fed an adequate diet of grain and other carefully-measured materials. Denied this the duck gets sick.

A duck does not live by corn alone, but by a carefully managed diet prepared by man.

ORGANISING YOUR DUCKS' DIET

Starter crumbs

It is not unusual for people to rear ducks from chicks, bought nine weeks before they are needed. This allows eight weeks to grow the birds, one to kill, dress and hang them. Consequently, the birds are first fed starter crumbs. Obviously, as the birds grow very quickly they need a lot of protein. This will give them good bones and solid meat. Starter crumbs, a balanced feed in chick-friendly crum form, are fed for the first month to five weeks of life.

Growers' pellets

In week six, pellets are used, with a growers' pellet which has reduced protein. Too much protein gives them gut problems and other ailments, such as stuck out feathers. These are the general pellets used for the bird's life, unless you put them on layers' pellets.

Important

Ducks will live quite happily, and lay lots of eggs on chickens' layers' pellets with one important proviso: they should never be fed any feed that has chicken medication in it. The coccidiant, for a start, is poisonous to ducks. You can cause your ducks all kinds of difficulties if you feed them medicated chicken food. However, you will find that if you keep hens and ducks together, they eat each other's food – so don't buy medicated feed. However, if you keep chickens and turkeys, you need medicated feed, so keep your ducks away.

FINISHER PELLETS

If you are growing ducks for meat then you will use these for a couple of weeks prior to killing. It gives them a bit of extra fat, they are healthier, and there is something final about it – preparing you for the deeds to come.

PROVIDING WATER

Try to give your birds two lots of water, one for drinking and the other for splashing in though to them it won't matter which they use for what. If there is a bowl or glug feeder for drinking water, all the better. Their splashing water can be separate. However, they will mess in both with equal abandon, and you should do your best to keep the water clean. I have used drip feeders with ducks.

ALLOWING YOUR DUCKS TO FORAGE

As we have said, foraging is important for ducks, nutritionally and socially. They are good at it and your garden will benefit so much more than with chickens who are a little more destructive.

But chickens are great at fighting dogs and cats – something which ducks are no good at really. Foxes, however will kill both hens and ducks, so you need to protect them. You really must protect your ducks from almost everything. Make their run cat-proof, or be sure the garden is as free from cats and dogs as you can make it.

OFFERING OYSTER SHELL

It's not always oyster, but you can buy mixed seashells in a bag which the ducks (and hens) will use to supplement their calcium intake. This in particular will give them good eggshells. Imagine all that calcium leaving the body every day – it has to be replaced. Their general diet gives them most of what they need but shell helps enormously.

All you have to do is pop it into a tray and the birds will do the rest.

MAKING GRIT AVAILABLE

The birds store grit in their gizzard and use this to paste their food with muscular action. When they are foraging they pick up some grit, but if they are confined to a run or for some other reason they cannot get grit, it is a good idea to have some available for them. You can buy specially graded grit, which is left out in a dish or tray for them to take as they feel like it.

PROVIDING EXTRAS

When you are sure your ducks have fed well on pellets, it is a good idea to give them some extras. They are fond of tomatoes, chopped greens and corn. Don't give them (actually, it's illegal) the scrapings from your plate; no meat or animal products except for chopped boiled hens' eggs.

Ducks don't like sloppy food, and generally I don't give them things like mash in the same way as I might with hens. I don't, for example, give them boiled potato too often, preferring to use drier foods.

CHAPTER 13

HOUSING DUCKS

It is possible to keep ducks with hens, but I would suggest you do not run them with geese. Geese are big birds, and while they are fine out in the field, a protective gander will attack anything he feels is a threat, and a few pecks will fatally damage your smaller birds.

Ideally, ducks should have their own house, and most of what has been said about chicken houses holds true for ducks. It is possible to house chickens and ducks together, but they need room. I have done it in a shed, and the roosting bars the chickens used were protected from the ducks by a large step they could not climb onto. This served to stop the hens accidentally pooing on the sleeping ducks beneath.

People who keep hens and ducks together often have an arc for each species, or a series of arcs, particularly if they wish to breed their birds, which you can do by placing birds of the same species or breed into arks together with the appropriate male, to get a clutch of fertile eggs.

The houses themselves need to be waterproof and airy. Ducks spend the whole of the day outside and usually only use the hut for roosting. They will take themselves off to bed in the evening and should be locked in.

MAKING THE HOUSING STRONG

The duck housing has to be strong. In my experience, foxes find ducks more easily than hens, though it is probably a close call as to more of which is eaten. But the housing is your responsibility, part of your duty of care, so make sure it is strong enough to withstand the antics of foxes, badgers and domestic dogs. If you can, make the housing secure from cats and dogs in the neighbourhood – they pee on the frames and it isn't all that pleasant for the inhabitants, and can put them off using it.

WATERPROOFING THE DUCK HOUSE

A plastic hen hut is always waterproof – and pretty much vermin-proof too. If the hut is wooden, it should at least have good-quality roofing felt as protection, preferably all around, so nothing can get inside. Ventilation should be, as for hens, high up and adequate to allow a constant change of air, without icy blasts.

Anyone looking at mallards in icy rivers will realise that ducks are quite good with cold, possibly better than hens, but they do not like wet and windy conditions, and having suffered the elements all day, they dry out and make themselves warm in the hut at night, so ventilate with some feeling for the ducks – don't make it into a wind tunnel!

SITING THE DUCK HOUSE

Place the hut in a sheltered spot, preferably not overhung by trees, since wild birds roosting in the trees poo into the hut and run, and this can spread disease. Protect the hut from cold, wet, icy winds in the winter and excessive heat in summer. I place an awning over the hut in the really hot days of summer to provide some shade.

LIFTING THE HUT

If possible, lift the hut by about six inches so that there will be no nesting rodents beneath. This leads on to the question of an entrance. Ducks waddle or walk (runners to be able to run, rather amusingly), but they don't hop or jump. So they will not cope with ladder entrances like hens do.

Ducks need a ramp that is at least a foot wide (30 cm) so they can slowly make their way into the hut. A step of only a few inches will cause ducks a real problem, so make sure the entrance and the ramp are continuous – they can simply waddle right into their roosting positions.

Don't feed your ducks in the hut, as they'll only mess it up completely.

ROOSTING

Ducks do not roost on poles like hens. I like to provide a grill for them to roost on, so that poo will fall through and can be cleaned away before there is a build-up and it doesn't settle (more or less) on their feet. The nature of duck poo is more liquid and possibly more corrosive than hens' poo. It is important to remove it as soon as possible. Very frequent cleaning of duck houses is necessary.

NESTING

This is a real problem. You provide a nest box and they don't use it, or they might one day but not another. They often prefer a corner where the bedding looks attractive.

It is good to provide a nest box, but you have to keep it clean, regularly removing bedding and always, every day, removing any eggs.

It is a good idea to watch your birds – probably the most important tip, actually. Try to find out, over time, which ducks are laying which eggs. This will tell you a lot about where they lay and you will see their routines. Sometimes a duck will lay just because she is ready, other times she will settle down having chosen her spot.

We have already said they lay in the early part of the morning, unlike hens who lay almost any time. It is best to keep them locked up until around 9 a.m. If you have to leave before then to go to work, then consider a trip home at lunchtime to collect the eggs.

FUMIGATING

Ducks suffer from the same set of mites as chickens are bothered by, though you don't get much in the way of red mite, although it *is* possible in mixed huts. They do get Northern Fowl mites, so you should change the bedding regularly. Watch out for aspergillosis (wheezing birds) if you use hay. I clean out every couple of days, because I don't like the smell of ammonia from their poo, and I am pretty sure they don't like it either. You can fumigate the hut by lighting a well-protected (no draughts, etc.) sulphur candle early in the day, after cleaning the droppings and bedding.

THE RUN

As with hens, if you are confining your birds to a run, and this makes sense in winter more than summer, then move them around every three months to keep the parasite loading as low as possible. Do not return to the same earth within six months. Ducks need a big run, and, to be honest, prefer the run of the garden.

You can keep ducks in place using only a low fence, around a metre or so high, but this will not do to keep predators out. It is best if your perimeter fence is secure from foxes, etc. A good hedge is best, but the weak spots are gates and so on. If you are at all worried, make the run fox-proof, which usually means having buried mesh and a roof.

CHAPTER 14

KEEPING DUCKS FOR EGGS

Duck eggs are delicious, possibly the most wonderful of all eggs, everywhere. They make the best cakes! They are about 20% bigger than the largest hens' egg, but as volume is a function of the cube power, there is an awful lot more 'stuff' in a duck egg.

Consequently, a laying duck has to be well fed and watered, free from stress and in good health. Ducks put a lot more into their egg production and are hungrier birds because of it.

CHOOSING DUCKS FOR EGG PRODUCTION

Laying ducks, of which the star has to be the Khaki Campbell, are called 'light ducks'. The Khaki Campbell will produce upwards of 300 eggs a year. It was produced by Adele Campbell who crossed an Indian Runner with a Rouen duck. The result was, more or less, the Khaki Campbell we see today, although she did some other crossing to enhance the colour.

You can see the mallard in the strain, it is a lovely shape and the duck is an excellent converter of food into eggs.

Most ducks, like chickens, come into lay at around 20 weeks, but ducks can often take somewhat longer, though they can be forgiven their tardiness because they lay so wonderfully.

The Khaki Campbell is an excellent duck for anyone wanting eggs. They are tolerant of both cold and heat and are readily available. Their adult weight is just under 2 kg – they are very active birds and great foragers. Pure-bred birds come in a number of shades of khaki, but look out to avoid examples that have either unusual stripes or seem very heavy.

The Indian Runner is the funniest of ducks – completely charming; they have such short legs, set far back in the pelvis so that they have to lean backwards at an angle in order to move at all. However, you will not be surprised to learn that, becaue the Khaki Campbell is such a prolific layer and is descended from the Runner that this breed is also a good layer.

Indian Runners lay about 200 eggs a year and they, too, are excellent converters of slugs and garden insects into egg. Much lighter than the Khaki Campbell, they weigh around 1.5 kg (that's a big one!) and do not fly. They do run fast though, and can often be seen running across the lawn emitting a barking quack.

Runners are less fastidious about where they lay their eggs, and you can find these all over the place (more about this later). It is said these ducks came from Bombay, but they have been bred all over the world, particularly in America. If you are keeping ducks for eggs, your life will be considerably lightened if you keep Indian Runners, if only for the fun of it. When they first appeared in the UK they were called 'Penguin Ducks', for obvious reasons.

WHAT'S THE EGG LIKE?

The shells are porous, thick and strong. They come in many colours – white, blue, green or a sort of dirty cream that some people describe as buff.

The duck egg has more fat in it than a hen's egg and the yolk is therefore very yellow. A fresh egg sits up when opened, the white is not runny and you get the impression something is holding it together – as though it has springs inside.

WHERE YOUR DUCKS LAY

Ducks will lay in the hut, in a nest box, most of the time. Increased sunlight causes them to start to lay and therefore most eggs are laid between dawn and about 9 a.m. For this reason, keep them locked in, if you can, until after breakfast and you should find the eggs inside.

What goes for chickens about pooing on the eggs also goes for ducks. They can mess on them, or have a small problem with the egg-laying apparatus inside (just the same as hens) and the egg may be smeared with either poo or blood. This is particularly so for birds that attract too much amorous attention.

Keep the hut clean, regularly changing the litter and moving manure. There need be no food or water inside, and your bedding has to be much cleaner than for chickens because the ducks are just as likely to lay in the middle of the floor as in a nest box.

Many breeds are apt to lay at any time, anywhere, and you have the problem of what to do with these eggs. Be sure to collect them as quickly as you can.

First, the shells are more porous than hens' eggs and poo can seep through. Second, mud (if the eggs are laid outside) can contaminate them. Also, when you wash the egg you can sometimes 'push' contaminants into the interior.

STORING DUCK EGGS

First of all, have a good rota, don't just have a pile of eggs and eat them willy-nilly. The porous nature of the shell makes them difficult to stop from becoming tainted if, say, they are stored with onions or garlic. Second, keep them out of the light and stack them with the pointed end down.

Keep them away from anything that might contaminate them, such as raw meat and cheese.

Keep them chilled, out of the light, which can cause the eggs to warm up, increasing the opportunities for microbial growth.

Duck eggs freeze quite well. Only freeze brand new fresh eggs by cracking them into freezer bags or even using ramekins. One person I know uses ice cube trays.

THE GOOD DUCK EGG GUIDE

- ▶ Keep everywhere clean, especially the hut.
- ▶ Keep ducks locked in until well into the morning.
- ▶ Collect eggs as soon as possible.
- ▶ Store in a strict rota, in a dark, cool place.
- ▶ Discard dirty and badly soiled eggs.

COOKING WITH DUCK EGGS

To be honest, I prefer to bake with them rather than have them boiled. I do not wish to provide recipes, but rather underline the precaution of eating the eggs, perhaps more important with 'home-grown' duck eggs.

Be certain to cook them properly – unfortunately no runny yolks – and a duck egg can take 7 minutes to cook. There is no doubt that cakes will turn out better with duck eggs because of the higher fat and protein content, and for this reason, if you do a lot of baking, keeping ducks for eggs is an excellent idea.

HOW DO DUCKS LAY EGGS?

The method is very similar to that of chickens. First, like hens, they do not *need* a male in order to lay. Unlike hens, however, ducks seem to be sad and they don't do so well without a male about. Ducks seem more cosy and settled when they are with a drake, however harsh he may be with them.

The duck ovary works exactly like that of a chicken, releasing an egg due to an impulse initiated by sunlight. The length of the day is also important.

The passage of the egg from the ovary to the outside world is exactly the same for a duck as for a chicken and the terminal portion of the gut and reproductive system work just the same, too.

Ducks have a number of eggs strung together and when these are finished the bird will moult. The moult is much quicker with ducks than with chickens, over in almost a week, when they can become all but bald in some cases and then grow a new set of feathers in a very short time.

Obviously, ducks go broody, too. There are many stories about ducks being bad mothers, but this is probably a little overemphasised. Certainly, if a broody duck is disturbed too often, she is in danger of just giving up, abandoning her eggs. However, should she be left alone, somewhere quiet, she will do a creditable job!

A broody duck is easier to handle than a broody hen: just put her out of the way and she will soon come round. One of the best ways of keeping a duck from broodiness is to constantly remove the eggs. An accumulation of eggs is tantamount to inviting the duck to try and hatch them.

CHAPTER 15

DUCK BREEDS

There are over 200 breeds of duck around the world, and obviously, you don't need that many in your back garden. The ducks that are generally useful to the small-time, or new, duck enthusiast are called Utility Breeds.

These can be good for both the table and egg production, but some of the birds in this list are prolific egg layers, too. Their names will be familiar to many because almost every county in the UK has its own utility breed. But many of them, like the agricultural shows that encouraged them, are dying out.

HOW TO BUY DUCKS

In essence this is very similar to buying chickens. There are a number of routes, some to be avoided, others being quite safe. The main point is, if you have no experience of ducks then do not think you can just read what follows and then go straight out and buy some birds.

To begin with, you should have everything ready for them before you start buying. This might sound obvious but in my youth I was buying rabbits at auction and coming home with ducks instead, because I just fancied them. Of course, it was terribly difficult accommodating them. Moreover, they were old ducks and didn't lay a single egg. But they were pretty. I suppose new, point of lay, ducks would have been equally pretty, and far more profitable.

If you lack experience, talk to someone who has it, and get as much advice and information as you can. For most of us this means buying ducks from a specialist supplier, and there are many of them on the internet. Go and visit them, and I would suggest the ones that give you the best information are the ones to buy from. Don't be too embarrassed to ask questions, and don't buy straight away.

To my mind this is the best way of buying ducks. Avoid the auctions until you are completely confident about what you are doing.

Joining a smallholding association is often another way of getting both information and birds. Finally, don't think that because you know about hens, you automatically know about ducks. You don't, though there are similarities. Make sure you prepare well before you start to care for them.

BUYING IN TRIOS

We have mentioned the fact that domestic poultry are social birds. While it is possible to keep hens without a cockerel, ducks do prefer a mate. It is standard to buy at least a trio of birds, preferably a drake and two ducks. If one of them dies there will still be another for company.

If your drake dies there is no hurry to replace him unless you really want ducklings. Two ducks will waddle round the garden very happily for a few months. Introduce a male very cautiously. Place all three in a pen where they can be seen and heard. Take steps to separate them if the new male is too violent. You're the boss, not the drake.

Introducing ducks into an established colony can be difficult, so take time over it. Put them in separate pens if necessary. Keep an eye on how they mix and then bring them together. Listen out for trouble in the hut and keep more than one feeding station.

CHOOSING YOUR DUCKS

Aylesbury

I can always hear Mr Toad remarking, 'An Aylesbury Duckling?' when someone accused him of looking like one in the snow. These are the white ducks that hail from Aylesbury in Buckinghamshire, but the truth is, this mallard-based breed comes from all around the midlands.

At one time these animals were bred as true utility birds, giving a reasonable carcass and egg production of around 150 a year. Unfortunately, this breed has suffered due to indifferent breeding, so if you are going to buy them, ask the seller to show you how good they are. Good ones will be expensive.

These birds eat quite a lot, and a good one will gain weight at an alarming rate. If you keep them as free range as possible, at least they will be able to work some of the excess off.

Pekin

This is another white type, based a couple of hundred years ago on a Chinese (surprise, surprise) duck. This is another dual-purpose breed that is easy to keep. They have tasty meat and lay around 160 eggs a year.

They are pleasant ducks, with laughing faces, and are slightly more runner-like than the Aylesbury. They are also slightly smaller than the Aylesbury, and a little busier about the garden, some would say 'flightier', and certainly they are able to fly, but only in short bursts. (You hardly ever see the Aylesbury take to the wing.) Pekins are certainly not as lazy and consequently do not grow so large.

They are not good mothers, so don't try breeding from them.

Khaki campbell
We have already looked at this breed briefly. She is an egg layer par excellence.

One of the things about these ducks is they are proud looking. They seem almost aristocratic with their heads held high. However, they make poor mothers. They will sit on the eggs, but usually a week and a half into the incubation, they become bored with the whole process and leave the eggs.

Increasingly difficult to find, these birds make good first-timers, but you have to be sure they are good layers, otherwise they are just one of the myriad cross-breeds and you end up with little more than slug-eating garden ornaments. Of course, there is nothing wrong with that, if that is what you want.

Muscovy
Most ducks have been bred from the mallard. Not so the Muscovy, possibly the least attractive bird bearing the name poultry. However, what they lack in looks they certainly make up for in character and friendliness. The name, Muscovy, means 'from Moscow', but these birds are really from South America, and have no links with Russia at all. To be honest, they look too Russian for my taste.

They have clawed toes and are sometimes referred to as the perching duck, because they will grasp a perch. They are large birds, comparatively, and often kept for meat, though they will lay 100 eggs or so a year.

Thankfully, if you like that sort of thing, Muscovies help to refute the reputation of ducks being poor mothers. They go broody often and make excellent mothers. You will get at least three broods a year with a trio, and soon have ducks everywhere. Removing the eggs straight away is important if you wish to prevent them being broody.

They are also excellent fliers, so don't forget to clip a wing, done exactly in the same way as for a chicken.

I have found Muscovies to like water rather more than most breeds, and if you can provide a larger splash bath – or better still a bit of a pond – they will be very happy indeed.

Indian runner

If you get a wine bottle and stick some funny legs at one end, you more or less have a runner duck. They came from the Far East, brought back by sailors – they were probably kept on board because they produced so many eggs.

These are comic birds, full of character, that run very rapidly with an amusing sway. They don't get very broody and rarely sit on eggs, so they make excellent back garden birds.

Generally, runners are healthier than most other birds, possibly because they are able to preen most of themselves with ease. They love water, and will splash much of the day. I am not sure their bodies are such that they cannot fly, but you certainly rarely see them on the wing.

If you were going to start off with a trio of anything, runners are the ones!

Call ducks

These are so small they are almost teal. They are pleasant little ducks which have all the habits of the bigger ones but need less space. They are very cute and excellent in the garden – especially where space is at a premium.

They are not terrific layers and are too small to be worth eating, but they are great first-timers. You certainly get a lot of duck in a small parcel.

They were used originally as decoys to bring down larger birds for shooting. The big problem is their noise. It is a coincidence that they are called 'call' ducks. The actual name comes from a Dutch word that means tethered or caged. But they do call quite a lot. Some describe it as being chatty, though your neighbours might have another name for it.

Rouen

This is the nearest you can get to a mallard. They are big, they fly, they don't lay many eggs – less than 100 a year. They are kept for three reasons: they are beautiful birds, they are reasonable mothers, and they have great meat. Maybe more than this, they have brilliant livers and your paté will be the best in the world.

KEEPING BANTAMS

Bantam hens, small versions of the main breeds, need almost as much room as their larger counterparts. But the bantam duck is much less flighty, and does well in a small garden. Often crossed with a call duck, they are calm, reasonable egg layers and certainly don't pad the grass into submission like a larger duck would.

Bantams produce eggs, smaller ones, of course, but full of fat and protein – which certainly make great cakes, and you get a reasonable number – 150 a year from many of them.

Everything said for large ducks holds true for bantams. They are fed, housed, watered and medicated in the same way – they're just smaller.

The major bantam breeds are the Black East Indian and the Silver Appleyard and you will have great success with either.

CHAPTER 16

DUCK DISEASES

On the whole ducks are a hardy lot, and do not succumb to much in the way of disease. Perhaps the most important point is to worm your ducks regularly and to delouse them, because they are prone to Northern Fowl Mite.

I don't wish to give you a long list of diseases; they'd only scare you to death at any rate. The simple rule of thumb is to watch and learn what is normal behaviour for your birds and then, if in doubt, call the vet. Normally, for 999 times out of 1000, your ducks will die either of old age or something more violent, followed by plucking and Sunday Lunch.

Keeping ducks healthy is more a matter of routine

TIPS FOR HEALTHY DUCKS

Good bedding
This should be preferably of the non-spore-bearing type such as straw, newspapers (shredded). It is important to change this very frequently so that your ducks always have good bedding to roost in and lay eggs in.

Good food
This means a balanced ration. Don't let them rely on foraging for food, never feed medicated chicken food, bread or corn as a main feed.

Safety and protection

Ducks suffer from stress, and when they are stressed, they start to get ill. Keep predators away from them, in particular, domestic cats which might not actually attack your ducks but will worry them just by hanging around.

Water

Always have good quality water available, both for drinking and splashing. This might mean changing it a couple of times a day. Ducks, like humans, don't do well if their drinking water is contaminated with poo.

Worming

We have already mentioned this, but it deserves mentioning a dozen times. A duck with worms doesn't grow, lay or resist disease as well as a duck without worms. The powder is simply poured over the feed – read the packet for dosing instructions.

A watchful eye

This is the best way to keep any livestock. Watch them, enjoy them. Look out for sluggishness, limping, shyness, excessive sitting and anything that you come to learn as unusual behaviour for that bird.

Young ducks

Always try to put new or young ducks on fresh pasture, one that has not been touched by other ducks or hens for at least six months.

A good vet

It is not always possible to find a vet that really knows about ducks. Ask questions as to whether they would welcome ducks, or if they would prefer if you went elsewhere. It can be distressing and expensive going to a vet who is not *au fait* with this slightly specialised bird.

Human hygiene

We must be sure we are not in danger from potential disease from ducks. Always wash your hands after cleaning out duck bedding, during which you should preferably wear rubber gloves and an overall, all of which which should be washed and disinfected after use.

When children have handled either the ducks, bedding, water, feed or eggs, make sure they also wash their hands. Get yourself and your children into the habit of wearing overalls, preferably gloves and definitely boots, wellington boots, that can be washed after use.

You won't want always to be wearing protective clothing. Be sensible, and when actually handling the ducks, wear the appropriate gear. A jumper full of poo can contaminate a lot of people over a day!

Bumblefoot

This is the most common problem with ducks. If a duck gets a small cut on the foot, bacterial infection can set in. This causes a swelling in the foot – often pus-filled, often hard, and the skin of the foot can crack. One of the ways of avoiding this is to have smooth, grassy runs, thus avoiding cuts to their feet. The treatment for such cuts is antibiotics, for which you have to go to the vet.

Viral enteritis

This is a disease caused by one of the herpes viruses. It comes more in mixed flocks; geese and swans get it, too. If your ducks wander, they can come in contact with a host of other ducks, and possibly catch the disease. A range of symptoms occur, from loss of appetite to drop in egg production, and tiredness.

Aspergillosis

This is a fungal infection which produces wheezing in birds. It is more of a problem with young ducks because it is slightly harder to clean the hutch, and they catch the fungus from the spores in the air.

The birds gasp and find breathing difficult, and they can quickly become dehydrated.

Make sure the litter and feed are always clean. Never allow them to become mouldy. Constantly refreshing litter and feed will keep this problem at bay.

Coccidiosis

Like chickens, ducks get these protozoan parasites which cause them to have a large number of splashes of blood in their poo. This problem is dealt with by using an appropriate treatment only available from the vet. The treatments for chickens are dangerous for ducks, so you have to treat them separately. It is a good idea to change pasture too, in such cases.

Worming

Most of the following worms are common to both hens and ducks, and a regular worming treatment (six monthly) and moving the run, will keep these at bay.

Gape worm

This is a worm that builds up in the trachea. If you get a bird, hen or duck, gasping, treat all your birds with the appropriate worming powder in the feed. They will soon clear up – but it is a good idea to move to fresh pasture.

Gizzard worm

The worms are found in the muscular part of the alimentary canal where food is ground. If you get red bits of blood in the poo, treat by worming.

Roundworms

You get tired birds with points of blood in the poo. The birds become generally run down and can fall prey to other diseases because their immunity is impaired.

External parasites

External mites and lice suck the duck's blood and lay eggs at the feather bed. This causes the birds to scratch and then the skin can be damaged, leading to other problems. Always treat mites, always clean out nest areas, bedding, houses, etc. so there is no build-up of problems.

It is not uncommon for ducks to be killed (old and young) by mites. If your duck is sitting on eggs she is particularly susceptible.

Flies

This is a common problem in sheep but ducks suffer from it, too. If you have loose-feathered ducks whose bottoms are messy, flies will lay eggs in the mess, and the maggots will eat through the poor animal's bottom. You can get powder for this, but always cleaning the animal's bottom, and even trimming the feathers is a great help.

Removal of eggs

When you treat your animals you will sometimes be required to discard the eggs. This withdrawal period is important to keep the medication out of the human food chain. Always read the packet and ask the advice of your vet.

PART THREE
BEES

CHAPTER 17

BEEKEEPING

There is something about the beekeeper that never struck home to me. Of all the rural activities, beekeeping is the most difficult to fathom. Not because it is difficult – on the contrary, it is easy – bees want to live as every organism does, and they will create their own little world in a series of boxes you provide for them.

I suppose the big problem is people. First of all, there is the dentist syndrome. We don't like little needles, and the same fear that makes the average Briton avoid the dentist keeps him from bees also. The beekeeper is held with almost medieval respect, a man (or woman) in touch with dark arts, secrets and special knowledge.

In my capacity as a trainer of beekeepers I have come across many tales of people wanting to get themselves into beekeeping only to be rebuffed by those in the know. Many is the time when novice beekeepers have come to me reeling from comments by some beekeepers that there is no room for such novices, that they are unwelcome, that they might only kill bees so what's the point.

Let me make one thing clear, well two things actually, but one of them should be obvious. First, anyone can keep bees. It is absorbing, sometimes taxing, but never out of reach. One of the aims of this section is to point out that beekeeping is not difficult and if you want to do it you jolly well should.

The other thing I want to make clear is that this book will not make you into a beekeeper. No book can. The idea behind this section is to give you enough information to see if you might at some time wish to keep bees. Hopefully it will encourage you along the path, help you to look at whatever space you have and decide if bees will fit in.

So you want to become a bee-keeper.

It is one of the fashionable things to do – keep bees. Around the country local beekeeping associations are struggling to get people onto courses, with demand outstripping supply many times over.

How many of the would-be beekeepers will end up with bees is not really known, but if you are one of those thinking about bees here are some of the things you need to know.

But, and it's a big but, there is a world of difference between reading a book about beekeeping and actually keeping bees. You might not, once surrounded by a thousand bees, be able to cope with such a large crowd of stinging insects and forget all the simple stuff you have read.

Again, it is one thing knowing the difference between a worker, a queen and a drone, but it's another thing altogether recognising the difference in real life.

You will need someone to hold your hand, to look at your space and help you fine tune it. You will need to be shown rather than just told how to use a smoker, what is going on in the hive, how to do the necessary tasks and treat for disease. How to help you when you get stung, how to prepare bees for winter and how to take honey.

In short – it's one thing reading a book, it's another thing actually doing it. But the doing of it isn't that difficult when you get down to it.

CHAPTER 18

BEE ANATOMY

This chapter isn't 'everything you need to know about a bee's insides'. Most of it is about the bee's outsides! You don't need to be an expert on bee anatomy to keep bees, but some understanding is useful.

All insects are sort of inside out in that the structure that keeps them together is on the outside, the exoskeleton. There are millions of species of insect, and this shows the success of the design. For example, bees have been around a long time, over 100 million years, although the social bees possibly a lot less, but it shows how successful the insect form is.

However, there are some major design problems with the insect form, which, should nature ever produce a solution, will doubtless bring bewildering life forms in the future.

THE RESPIRATORY AND CIRCULATORY SYSTEM

Bees do not have lungs. Instead a system of tubes take air from pores in the sides of the insect. The holes are called spiracles, and the transport of gasses in and out of the insect is very inefficient. The tubes end deep in the bee and are surrounded by bee blood, also known as haemocoel. Oxygen enters the tissues and carbon dioxide leaves via these tubes.

This inefficient system is the single reason why these bees are not much bigger, like those you see in some comics.

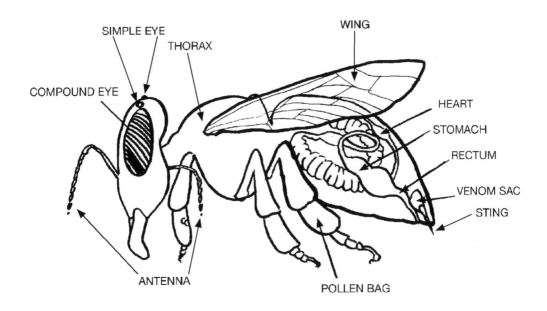

SIMPLE EYE
THORAX
WING
COMPOUND EYE
HEART
STOMACH
RECTUM
VENOM SAC
STING
ANTENNA
POLLEN BAG

These tubes can become blocked and consequently the bee cannot breathe. You see them walking around with their wings in a 'K' shape. The disease acarine is one such case, a mite enters the spiracles and lays eggs. The grubs grow to fill the pores and the bee dies.

Equally inefficient is the circulatory system. There is a dorsal (along the back) blood vessel that has a number of 'hearts' along its length, and a few branches, but there are few capillaries and often the tissues are simply bathed in the liquid. The circulation is very simple and often too slow to provide enough oxygen all around the animal.

Sometimes, after a flight, bees will simply sit and expand and contract their abdomens as best they can to get as much air and blood flow as possible.

THE EXOSKELETON

This is a marvellous array of plates that overlap at the edges. The plates resemble a Roman soldier's shield, overlapping and hinged, and are called *terga*. They are linked together to form a *scutellum*, or shield. Each plate is covered in wax and made from the hard protein, chitin. In this way the bee is encased in an armoured suit which, because of its wax coating, does not dry out.

The exoskeleton forms a great defence, although the bees can be stung by other bees and wasps at the joints of the plates.

The plates move in relation to each other, but do not grow. Once a bee is adult, it is stuck in its body and will not grow any more.

The (internal) muscles are attached to the plates, so movement comes from *within* the skeleton, unlike in humans.

WINGS AND LEGS

Obviously the bee has the typical insect architecture of head, thorax and abdomen. The thorax is made of three segments, the abdomen of nine.

The three segments of the thorax have only two pairs of wings but three pairs of legs.

The legs are really important because they are more than just organs of locomotion. They contain sensors to chemicals, sound and vibration. Bees hear through their legs.

The final pair of legs, the backmost, has a comb that collects pollen and is known as the pollen sac. You see bees coming into the hive with pollen attached to their back legs. Each bee collects the same pollen, putting it into the same cell in the hive. You therefore get different coloured honeys, each in their own cell. It looks quite remarkable, all the various colours of pollen from creamy white to deep yellow and almost every other colour you can think of.

The bee's wings are amazing. They act like a very complex helicopter and the orientation of the wings can move the animal in any number of ways. The outer edges of the wing tips are covered in hairs and allow the wings to act singly or in conjunction with its partner. Quite clearly insects invented velcro a long, long time before us.

THE HEAD

The reason for a complicated brain in the head is simple – that's where the eyes are. The information passed from the compound eye is processed in the ganglia of the head. The eyes are made up of thousands of cells, each creating a single image, often only of one point of light. On the whole the bee responds to changes in light. As a cell sends its message to the brain, the bee can act instantly. There are also some little eyes on the top of the head called *ocelli*. All insects have them (spiders have more), but in bees they are used to detect quick changes of light such as a shadow falling over the bee. These are triggered when you open the hive, or stand over a bee.

The head also has the bee tongue and mouth parts with which the bee nibbles at wax, through flowers if it can't get to the nectar, through paper in the hive when you are joining two colonies, at the wood of the frames and in making wax or laying down propolis.

The tongue, or proboscis, acts as a sponge, drawing up nectar on contact and is shielded by some special mouth parts which make it a little like a straw.

The antennae are collections of hairs and tissues loaded with chemo receptors. Once a certain chemical 'fits' into its respective place, it sends a message to the ganglia. The bee knows where it is largely by tasting. Special receptors allow hormones from the queen to maintain the bee's physiology. For example, the queen releases a hormone (strictly speaking, hormones meant for outside of the body are caller pheromones) that stops the bee from having the urge to make queen cells.

The bee's head is full of glands. There are hypopharangeal and mandibular glands that produce royal jelly and bee food.

INSIDE THE BEE

Nectar is transferred into a portion of the alimentary canal called the honey stomach. Here, enzymes are mixed with the nectar, converting some of the complex, disaccharide sugars into more simple ones.

When the bee returns to the hive it regurgitates the material into a cell, and the other bees work on it. In a way, honey is bee vomit.

Some of the nectar passes through the rest of the intestine. The bee intestine is amazing. In the winter those bees in the hive with the queen can store up loads of waste so they don't have to go outside the hive to poo.

The waste produced by the bees is collected into kidney-type organs called malpighian tubules which empty into the gut.

THE STING

This is a modified ovipositor (for laying eggs) which has its own blood supply and its own 'heart'. The whole thing ends in a sharp needle with a barb in it. When the bee stings, the act of flying away (or of being knocked away with an expletive) causes the whole mechanism to be pulled out. You can see the venom sack pulsating. If you grab at it with your fingers you are likely to squeeze all the venom into the wound. The thing to do is slide it out with your hive tool, thus lessening the dose (see page 123).

DIFFERENCES BETWEEN THE CASTES

Of course, there are differences between bees. The queen has big ovaries, and a place to store sperm. How she keeps sperm throughout her life is down to her ability to feed it. She can release a single sperm at a time, something I find truly amazing.

The queen also has a sting, but never uses it on humans, only on other queens, and it is never torn from her abdomen.

One of the truly amazing things about bee organisation is that drones do not have a sting! We have already said that the workers expel drones before the winter – if they had stings, they would fight back!

CHAPTER 19

GETTING STARTED

It takes a little nerve for someone new to beekeeping to set out along the path that leads to your own first full jar of golden honey. But it's an exciting path to tread, where you will learn a lot about the wonderful world of the bee and not a little about yourself in the process.

ASKING FOR ADVICE FROM EXPERIENCED BEEKEEPERS

Perhaps the most important advice anyone can give an aspiring beekeeper is to meet with others already involved in the hobby. This way you will be able to get hands-on experience and get a feeling for how you will react when around bees. Beekeeping societies are to be found in almost every town, and you will be most welcome at their meetings and demonstrations.

I cannot overemphasise the importance of getting some experience around bees before you take the plunge. I would like to tell you about myself.

My first bees were a swarm. A friend brought them to me – he was a beekeeper, and plonked them in a box for me. I was watching from the safety of my greenhouse, with all the windows and the door firmly shut.

My friend closed the hive and went away, patting me on the back as he went. I didn't have a bee suit, but I made for myself a smock out of a Norwegian Army snow suit, the hood of which I sewed in with some netting. It was very thick and very hot. Underneath this I wore a thick jumper and two pairs of trousers.

I bought a smoker and took hours lighting the thing. I opened my hive for the first time, looking like a Michelin Man and I was wearing the thickest gloves I could find.

I inspected the frames and found myself covered in bees, my arms and particularly my back. I was breathing heavily and very hot. After only a few seconds, I unceremoniously dumped the frames back into the hive, plonked the lid on and ran. I was scared of not knowing what I was doing, not understanding what I saw before me, of being stung, of killing the bees, of being sick right into the brood box (I wonder what that would have done for varroa control?).

It is quite natural to be feeling all these things, but it is probably best – definitely best – if you can get over nightmares of beekeeping with someone who knows what he is doing.

WEARING PROTECTIVE CLOTHING

Whenever you think of beekeeping the picture of someone dressed in a white suit with a net over the head to keep the bees off. You can cover up as much as you like and the addition of a good pair of beekeeping gauntlets keeps you totally safe from stings unless you catch a bee in a crease somewhere and it stings you when you get undressed.

It is the ubiquitous bee suit that everyone buys, and they do protect. By all means wear gauntlets, but you will find, after going into the hive a couple of times, they are a bit cumbersome. A stout pair of washing up gloves does the job just as well (an expensive pair, not the cheap ones). But even then you will eventually find yourself using just your skin.

There is something to be said for getting stung. It's painful – yes. But when you have had a few stings, it is not so bad. Actually it's OK, yes it hurts, but not that badly.

Always wear boots and never go into the hive without a veil. You are not proving anything by it, and (as I can testify) a bee in the ear is a real pain to get out – and a sting in the eye or up a nostril is just a nightmare.

USING A SMOKER

Another important piece of equipment, the smoker, burns grass, moss, peat, newspaper, bark and cardboard slowly; almost anything that can burn – and probably the best material to burn, if you can get it, is old sacking.

Bees evolved in woodland and you can trick them into thinking there is a fire by smoking them. When they detect smoke, first of all they move away from it and then they gorge themselves on honey in preparation to escape. When you use the smoker, most of the bees fill up to bursting point making it difficult for them to sting.

It doesn't *stop* them from stinging, as you will find out, but it does help.

The best use for the smoker is simply to move bees away, as they will retreat into the body of the hive. This is most important when reassembling the hive and putting the crown board in place. You kill fewer bees if you have smoked them away.

Lighting the smoker

It is difficult to start a fire down a tube! I personally use some paper and a long gas-powered lighter – the kind used for lighting cookers. Gently puff the bellows and get the paper alight then pop more paper on top of this until you get a good blaze going. On top of this add your combustible material, while puffing away. Pretty soon it will all be alight, and you can close the lid.

Remember, the smoker is hot! Pick it up carefully and only buy one with a guard. It will also need replenishing, so don't let it go out. There is nothing worse than reaching for your smoker and finding it has gone out.

Sacking will burn for ages – keep giving it a little puff now and then to be sure it's going.

If you only have one hive, it will last the ten minutes or so you are in there – but more than one presents fuelling problems. Always make sure you have enough smoke for the hive before you open it up.

Using the smoker
You always only give one puff – you are not John Wayne, flame throwing the baddies in a film. Be gentle. Before opening, give a little puff at the entrance. This tells the bees there is something happening and many will get honey.

Remove the lid and give another puff under the crown board.

Then only smoke when you have a lot of bees around, otherwise you will hinder the process. Smoke with a sweeping movement using a single puff of the bellows. Don't repeatedly pull at the smoker; it gets hot and you can get flames firing out of the funnel. All you need is gentle smoke.

When reassembling the hive, use gentle smoke to move the bees from the edges of the hive.

I don't like using smoke. It makes my throat dry and I am sure the bees are also affected by it. I use it only if I really have to.

BUYING A HIVE TOOL
This looks like a chisel. You use it to move frames, lifting them out when they are glued tight by the bees, and to remove queen cells. It is the most organically-shaped tool in the farming world.

There are various jobs that the hive tool is important for. There are many designs, too. I prefer the one with a curled end – it allows me to get under the lips of the frames and lever them out, the bees having glued them together.

Another job is the removal of combs from the bars of the hive. Bees will make a lot of wax on the frames, which I always remove because it can glue up the whole hive, affect the queen excluder, allowing the queen to wriggle through if it is bent.

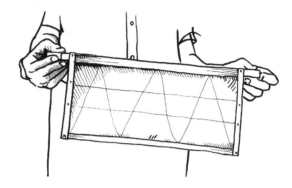

The other use of the hive tool is the collection of propolis, which the bees use for gluing. Propolis is a wonderful material which the bees collect from trees and add enzymes to. It is their glue, and it has fantastic antiseptic qualities. A solution in alcohol keeps viruses at bay – no more sore throats. A word of warning – it stains so badly that you will never get it out of your clothes!

Using the blade side of the hive tool, there is one problem. If you have not made your frames properly then any pins protruding from the top of the frame will take a chunk out of your hive tool – or your finger come to that!

USING BUCKETS

A bucket for disinfecting your tools
If you have more than one hive you need a way of cleaning your utensils before you go into the next one. Yes, bees rob from each other, and consequently can spread disease from one colony to another, but your hive tools and hands can do this more effectively.

A bucket of water with a handful of washing soda and some detergent in it will do for both hands and tools.

Another bucket for collecting wax

This one is for all those bits of wax you collect from the hive. Don't just throw them about on the floor, keep them apart and take them home. Get into the habit of being completely clean about the hives. Other bees can smell wax (and so can wasps) and will then come and rob your bees. It can be a problem if a strong colony robs from a weak one, as the weak one can die as a result. Almost universally, however, robbing bees bring disease, viruses and a lot of other problems.

Never leave bits of hive products, wax and so on, honey or dead bees about the hive – always take them away.

BLOWTORCH

This is an important tool for removing germs and infectants in wooden hives. The wood of an old hive is made suitable for use for another colony by blowtorching it. The heat kills everything that could cause problems in the new colony. You have to flame all the surfaces of the hive, melting the wax and propolis until it boils.

FEEDERS

When you take honey from the hive (and I always leave a super (see page 129) full of honey for the bees) you should feed them. A feeder is a useful tool for beekeepers, and there are many designs of feeders. They can fit in the lid of the hive, or in a super, and you fill them with ordinary white sugar syrup.

The concentration of the sugar is important. If you make 1:1 syrup, that is, 1 kg sugar to 1 litre of water, it will encourage the bees to fly. For autumn and spring feeding, when you don't particularly want them to fly, make a 2:1 syrup – 2 kg sugar to 1 litre of water.

In the winter make (or buy) some fondant. This is placed on the top bars of the frames and the bees eat into it. You make fondant a bit like making jam (well only a bit) by using 4 parts sugar to 1 part water. A teaspoon of vinegar per litre of water will help break down some of the sugar.

Fondant recipe

Pour sugar, water and vinegar into saucepan and bring to the boil stirring constantly.

Cover and gently boil up for about five minutes.

Remove lid and check temperature with cooking thermometer, continue to boil with lid off until temperature reaches 112°C/(234°F).

Remove from heat and cool to 93°C/(200°F).

Whip with a mixer (preferably electric) until the mixture begins to turn white and creamy with air bubbles.

Pour into shallow setting pans.

Allow to cool undisturbed.

To feed bees, place inverted pan on top of frames.

Feeders allow the introduction of medicine into the hive, by adding it to the feed. Fumidil B is a case in point, which is used for treating the protist infection nosema.

VARROA CONTROL REQUIREMENTS

You will need to buy different treatments for varroa control. We are no longer allowed to treat with insecticides, as the mites are becoming immune to it. However, Thymol strips are often used in the winter, oxalic acid pouring in the dead of winter. Icing sugar is used in the middle of the year. More of this later.

CHOOSING THE HIVE

There are lots of designs of beehives. When you think of the traditional beehive, it has lapped sides and is almost invariably white. These, called WBC after its designer, William Broughton Carr, are actually made of two parts. The outside hoops of wood conceal an inner box hive that is used today alone, as the British National Hive. The hoops are little more than a nuisance, having to be removed before the hive itself can be examined.

The British National is largely only used in the UK, and all kinds of different sizes of hives exist – usually not interchangeable with each other.

Most commercial beekeepers use a large hive called the Langstroth, an American design named after its designer, an eminent Victorian beekeeper, the Reverend Langstroth.

You can buy hives made from polystyrene and a number of plastic designs are available. For the most part this section will concentrate on British National Hives, made from wood, but most of what is said applies equally to plastic hives, except the need for flaming.

Plastic hives cannot be flamed – they melt! However, they can be fumigated by using disinfectant – Domestos, for example, works brilliantly.

A modern, productive beehive consists of two or more boxes. The lower box, or brood box, sits on what is referred to as a varroa floor. This is simply an open mesh, through which varroa mites fall having been knocked off by cleaning bees or simply by chance. As they fall out of the hive, they cannot climb back again. The varroa floor accounts for a reasonable reduction in mite population. Yesteryear beekeepers used a solid floor, but the mites were found to climb back inside again. A white plastic sheet beneath the floor allows you to keep a count on the numbers of mites falling through. This then will give you an estimate as to how many mites are inside the colony.

This floor provides an entrance to the hive for the bees at the bottom. The floor sticks out a little at the front, forming an 'alighting table', where the bees land and take off when foraging, though the kind of alighting tables you used to get when solid floors were in use are long gone.

The entrance to the hive is usually about a centimetre across, and is used for ventilation as well as getting in and out of the colony.

Unfortunately other animals use the entrance. Wasps are good fighters and the bees cannot defend a full 46 cm gap, so the entrance is constricted for the late summer and into the autumn to about 3 cm – giving them a fighting chance against wasp attack.

Similarly, in the winter, mice can rob the hive, so a mouse guard is used. It is amazing how small a space a mouse can creep through.

THE BROOD BOX

This forms the largest part of the hive, and holds a number of frames that each have a honeycomb of wax on them. The queen is restricted to this area and lays her eggs in the cells that the workers produce and clean out. She would happily lay all over the hive given the chance, but is prevented from doing so by a special grill, called the 'queen excluder'. The queen excluder fits on top of the brood box. Fat with eggs, she's unable to squeeze between the wires of the excluder into the higher boxes, although the workers can easily pass through. As they find the cells in the higher boxes free from eggs, they simply store honey in them instead.

The frames in the brood box are deep and, having been made up by the workers, are ready for the queen to lay her eggs in the cells. A good pattern of laying is indicative of how well the queen is doing. Normally a consistent laying pattern, with few 'pepperpot' empty cells, and a band of honey stores above is what you are looking for.

The brood box in a National hive holds 9, 10 or 11 frames – you decide. Sometimes the frames simply rest on a runner in the box, and are set at the correct space by the shape of the frames. Other arrangements have metal castellations at the top of the box, into which the frames slot.

REARRANGING THE FURNITURE

When you go into the brood box, first, you have to be gentle: don't bash the frames around – you might kill the queen. Second, brood boxes have to be returned in the correct order and in the same position. Mixing them up or putting them back the opposite way round is like someone breaking into your house and changing the walls, the rooms and the furniture. It confuses the bees.

THE SUPERS

These are the boxes that are piled on top of the brood box, separated by a single queen excluder. (You only need one queen excluder per hive – most of the time.) There may be as many as four or five supers, but usually there are two. The frames in the supers are smaller than those in the brood box. When the honey has matured in the cells, mature workers come along and cap them with wax.

When a super is full of honey it weighs 15 kg, and you can remove a super from the bees having removed the bees from the super.

A board, called the crown board, is placed on top of the supers, closing off the top of the hive. This can have a bee trap, called a Porter Bee Escape, allowing bees to get out but not in, forcing them to return via the bottom of the hive. In this way you can empty the bees from the super box if you put a blank board beneath the box and a crown board fitted with a bee escape at the top.

THE LID

On top of the hive is a substantial but loosely-fitting lid that's completely waterproof. Pitched roofs are more waterproof than flat ones, but less useful when it comes to stacking. You can up-turn a flat lid and place the supers and brood boxes on it as you inspect your hive.

THE STAND

The hive stand is an important piece of equipment. First of all it allows the boxes to be at the correct height for easy manoeuvring. Beekeeping can be heavy work and the boxes are more easily moved if they are at a suitable height.

Second, it is good to be able to attach the hive to something solid. This is especially important if the hives become disturbed by wildlife or humans.

The whole hive is held together with a tension belt, the kind used by hauliers when transporting goods. If you have fixed your stand to a solid surface, or buried it in the ground, you will then be able to secure the whole structure with the belt.

Make sure the belt is well-oiled. They can rust easily, and become impossible to undo!

A MENTOR

To avoid problems, and to help you through the process of keeping bees you need support – a beekeeping mentor. Often one can be found by going first to a local beekeeping association. Many of them have courses, but you will probably find many of them are booked up for some time. However, ask to become a member. It brings not only insurance but also expertise, friendship and help.

You will go into a hive under supervision many times during your training but you will find a time when doing it by yourself when you need help and advice.

You might need someone to come along and tell you (or remind you) what to do. And when you can't find a queen and there are queen cells on the frames, just what should you do? You need a friendly mentor to help you through everything.

RACES OF BEES

People who do not know the difference among bees regard them all as being the same. They confuse honeybees with bumblebees. They believe bumblebees give honey. They think honeybees live underground. Most interestingly, you find photographs of bumblebees illustrating honeybee articles in newspapers and magazines.

Around the world there are a number of races of honeybees. Each has its own characteristics and the beekeepers interbreed them to produce bees suitable for their local climate and predominant floral conditions. It's likely that any bees you keep will be hybridised to some degree.

The original bee in the UK was the British Black, which died out 100 years ago. It has been replaced by hybrids, such as the Buckfast Bee, bred to replace the British Black. There are many other races from around the world, perhaps the most common in the UK being the Italian *Apis meliffera linguistica.*

CASTES OF BEE

Bee society is fairly complex and consists of three types of bee: the queen, female workers and male drones. The bees live together as a colony. In a way, the colony is a single organic entity and the individual bees only a part of this.

Queen

The queen controls the hive in only this respect. She emits hormones that give the colony its own distinct aroma which all the bees recognise, so they attack any bees coming from a different hive. The hormones give the colony its identity, and the strength of the hormones is proportional to the fertility of the queen. When the queen is failing, due to age or perhaps sickness or injury, the workers will replace her by feeding royal jelly to a suitable egg.

It's the queen's job to lay eggs. Over her short life she will lay many thousands of eggs to give the colony a chance to collect enough food for the winter, and make enough bees to reproduce in the spring. Apart from these important functions, it is the workers that have overall control of the colony.

Queens are made in cells called 'queen cells'. Depending on the state of the old queen these cells are usually found at the bottom of a brood box frame – in which case they are called Reproduction or Supersedure cells. If the queen is sick or injured the workers will produce emergency queen cells in the middle of the frame.

Either way the queen has produced her own replacement and the egg, a fertilised egg, is fed royal jelly to develop its ovaries and fertility. The young queen (or queens in a swarming hive) will emerge to be mated by drones. She will mate with a dozen or so males, a courtship that will last possibly a couple of days.

An older colony will produce several queen cells, and beekeepers have to decide what to do about them. If all the queens hatch the colony may swarm, something of a disaster in the early summer. But, at some point the old queen will run out of eggs to lay and a new queen will then be needed. A queen never lasts more than five years, and usually is only allowed to live for three at most. Re-queening is a straightforward process, which allows the colony to be replenished. More importantly, part of the beekeeping process is about increasing your stock.

Usually, when you buy a colony, or if you buy a queen, she will come with a mark on her back, painted by the originator. The colour of the mark represents the year she was produced. The colour represents the ending of the year, so a white mark says the bee was produced either in 2011 or 2006, but since we never keep queens for more than 5 years, she was produced in 2011. There will not be another white queen until 2016.

The sequence is:

White: 1 or 6
Yellow: 2 or 7
Red: 3 or 8
Green: 4 or 9
Blue: 5 or 0.

Workers

The worker bee (an infertile female) is by far the most numerous member of the hive. They live for around 66 days and start their lives as a fertilised egg in an area in the hive called the 'brood box'. When they emerge as a bee, around 22 days after hatching they start their brief but productive life by cleaning the frames and then progress to other duties as they grow older. These include ventilating, guarding and cleaning the hive, and feeding the queen. This takes up the second period of 22 days, and when they are ready they spend the final 22 days foraging. They literally work themselves to death flying thousands of miles collecting nectar to be converted into honey.

At the height of summer, a hive may contain 40,000 bees. It's the workers that collect nectar, water and pollen. When they return from finding a new food source, its position is communicated to the other foraging bees by the performance of a dance, called a 'waggle' dance. The workers make many decisions about foraging, about protecting the hive and the life in the hive.

They also act as nursemaids, feeding the grubs, and storing pollen and honey. And, when they are older, they secrete the wax from which honeycomb is made. Foraging bees collect a substance from trees and plants called propolis. They use this to glue up the hive – they love glueing! Propolis has really powerful antiseptic properties and is used to keep the hive free from many bacteria. Possibly the most important thing about it is that it keeps out draughts!

Workers also make new queens by feeding them 'royal jelly', a substance secreted from their hypopharyngeal gland. This occurs in response to the age or the health of the current queen.

Drones

There are also a relatively small number of male bees, called drones, who only have one job: to mate with a new queen when she goes on her nuptial flight. In May or June they fly off to locations where they are joined by a virgin queen. The queen will mate with around ten drones during this flight and the sperm she collects will last all her life.

Drones are larger than workers and a little smaller than the queen. They have no sting. They start life as an unfertilised egg.

Having mated, the successful drone dies and all the rest return to the hive where the workers throw them out at the end of the summer to die. No matter how hard they try to gain access, the drones are forcibly evicted time and again until all have died.

Drones are sacrificed by beekeepers in order to cut down the number of varroa mites in the colonies. If you allow workers to make drone combs, varroa mites prefer to enter the larger drone cells. When these cells are capped by the workers, they can be removed by the beekeeper, taking a large proportion of mites with them.

HOW TO BUY BEES

My first bees came to me because of the beekeeping association of which I had become a member. I made friendships, and good beekeeping is about friendships. The association had an apiary and in the late spring I was offered a swarm, which cost me nothing, and I got a mentor at the same time.

This is without doubt the best way to acquire bees. Of course, you can also go to all kinds of lengths to buy colonies, mostly in the spring, mostly supplied as nucleii.

The nucleus

This is a small box that holds five frames of brood. Right now you can pay up to £200 for a 'nuc'. The frames from a nuc should be placed in the centre of a hive, and they should be fed with 2:1 syrup that is two parts sugar to one part water.

There are many companies who will sell you starter kits or actual bees. You should have no difficulty in raising these bees as long as you get them early in the season, and make sure they collect plenty of honey for themselves.

You will not know anything about the origin of these bees, so check for varroa and, at the same time, add some Fumidil B to their feed. It would be a good idea to invite your local bee inspector to have a look at them, too.

Buying a queen

Many people sell queens, which come in little plastic cages with a few attendant workers. If you can beg/borrow or buy three frames or maybe four of bees in a nucleus box, you can add the queen cage to them. The first intent the workers have is to kill the queen because they are not her workers and they don't smell the same as she does. However, the bottom of the queen cage is plugged with candy. By the time the workers have eaten through the candy, they smell of the new, introduced queen and they usually accept her. There is a chance of failure, but at only £25 per queen, this represents a cheaper option. In order to persuade someone to give you three frames of brood usually means joining an association: I cannot stress this too much – join an association!

CHAPTER 20

THE BEEKEEPING YEAR

Beekeepers talk about cycles, which is essentially how long it takes bees to emerge for foraging. You can take this as 22 days. A young bee will take 22 days to emerge from being an egg and grub and a further 22 days to emerge to forage.

This can be said to start in the spring when the queen begins to lay eggs and the number of bees in the hive builds up. Remember, it takes 44 days for eggs laid to start to forage for food. This means the bees have to time the increase in numbers as flows of nectar and pollen arrive in the spring. Often, apple is the first pollen in the spring. Bees will collect pollen in order to feed grubs, and if there is none available in the hive the bees can have a poor start to the year.

As more plants come on tap, the bee numbers increase to take advantage of the nectar that is flowing (it sounds almost like the brewery tap!).

The queen lays an increasing number of eggs each day.

By March there is frequently a large number of new bees, each consuming food that is not necessarily being replaced. In this case, you need to be sure the colony doesn't starve. Make some fondant (see page 126) or buy it and pop it into the hive very quickly so you don't chill any young.

In April the colony is growing. Choose a warm day (around 15°C) and make sure there is space in the hive for the expanding colony. Add a feeder with 1:1 sugar and water, which will not only feed the colony, but will encourage workers ready to fly.

By May you are not only hoping the colony is growing, but that it also has plenty of room to expand. You may find a lot of drones and a queen cell, and you must be prepared to do something about it.

You should inspect the colony weekly and check for swarming possibilities. Move old brood frames at the outside out of the hive and replace them with new ones. Try to replace at least four frames each year. Do not reuse the old frames – pull them apart, harvest the honey and flame the old wood before reassembling it with a new foundation.

Add a super, especially if the current one is full.

We will talk about swarming in the next chapter, but at this point the hive will be ready to reproduce itself.

There is an old poem:

A swarm in May's worth a bale of hay
A swarm in June is worth a silver spoon
A swarm in July isn't worth a fly.

May and June are the most important times for swarming, and you should consider having something available to catch swarms, e.g. a bait hive on a shed roof, even if you have undergone artificial swarming.

By June and July your supers will be filling with honey. This is an exciting, if scary, time. The bee numbers will be peaking around now and you will have the largest numbers of varroa mites, too. We will look at varroa in Chapter 22, but the brood box should be as full as possible, and the mite numbers will also be high. Consider drone brood sacrifice or the use of icing sugar. You might be able to take a crop of honey, either a few frames or even a full super. Remember to replace frames as they are taken.

In August you can remove supers of honey for extraction. You need to leave some for the bees, and I normally give them a whole super for themselves. If there was one super of honey, and you have removed it, put the empty frames back once you have extracted the honey. If you do this in early August, they will probably have completely replaced it by the middle of September. If not, add frames of their own honey to make up a full super.

In late August the bees are treated for varroa again. You might have dusted them with icing sugar in July or August and used drone sacrifice again too. In late August, Thymol is used. In the middle of winter, when the bees are at their lowest number, a treatment with oxalic acid is often used to get the varroa mites down to their lowest numbers.

After the harvest and the varroa treatment, the bees are prepared for winter. Hopefully they will have a full super of honey and some feed – 2:1 feed – which can continue until early October. After that use fondant to feed the bees, which is placed in the shallow tin you made it in or without, so the bees can easily get to it. You can add Fumidil B to the September feed to treat the colony against nosema.

The mouse guards are fitted to the entrance and with plenty of food the bees are locked up.

WARM WAY/COLD WAY

The boxes can be arranged so the frames face either parallel to the entrance or perpendicular to it. Imagine frames perpendicular to the entrance – there is no resistance to draughts, and this is known as the cold way. If you arrange the box so the wind is stopped by the first frame, this is known as the warm way. I always arrange the boxes the warm way in winter.

The bees should be left undisturbed until the middle of winter, when you treat with oxalic acid.

Remember, other problems can arise, the hive might be pushed over by people or animals, so secure it. They might be attacked by woodpeckers and badgers. Make sure the hive is as sturdy as possible.

Keep some fondant available for emergency feeding.

THE DEVELOPMENT OF BEES

We will look at the worker bee and call her typical. The queen is quite an exception and is dealt with in the next section.

Worker bees, infertile females, live for 66 days on average, except those that overwinter in the hive, who have a torrid time keeping warm with dwindling food resources.

The first days are spent as an egg. This is vertical in the cell on day 1, less so on day 2 and by day 4 they are flat on the base of the cell. Within a few days they have become a grub and are fed a substance called 'bee bread' by the nursery workers, plus a few enzymes and hormones.

From day 4 to about day 9 the grubs are open in the cells and they are attended by other bees until it is time for them to pupate. Around day 9 the bees put a wax seal on the cells and inside the bees pupate, emerging on day 22.

For a few days they find their way around the colony – where the food is, where the water and queen are. They lick the queen and make themselves fully a part of the colony.

They emerge with hairs all over them which get rubbed off as they bump around the brood.

During this second period of 22 days the worker bee doesn't leave the hive. She first starts to feed grubs and the queen, tidies up around the brood, removes dead bees – general housekeeping, so to speak. She then takes on board the duties of wax secretor, and makes up the comb and cells. Then the worker bees become ventilators and guard bees at the entrance. This is the last of their household duties and they soon make themselves ready for the next stage.

ORIENTATION FLIGHTS

Worker bees, 44 days old, fly out of the hive and take a memory photograph of where they are. They do the same at differing heights and this builds up a memory of where they live. Having worked this out they are embedded with this information. They will fly up to 2 miles, always returning to the hive. If you move the hive more than a few feet the bees will return only to where the hive was.

The rule is: move the hive less than 2 feet or more than 2 miles.

During this last period of 22 days the bee will fly thousands of miles in pursuit of nectar, water, pollen and propolis. She will wear herself out collecting enough nectar for just a teaspoon of honey.

CHAPTER 21

BEEKEEPING TECHNIQUES

There are not a lot of techniques to master when you are thinking about keeping bees. Probably the most important technique, and this relates to all animal husbandry on a small scale, is to develop the ability to like and enjoy what you are doing. Consequently, gaining an empathy, a feeling for your bees is an important part of beekeeping.

Second, the ability not to panic is important too. You will, at some point in your career, be covered with bees, have them flying around your head and not really know what you are doing or looking for, but the ability to keep calm, reassemble the hive and walk away from your bees is all you really need in such circumstances.

You need to have the ability to deal with a sting without fuss – keep calm and carry on.

WHAT ARE YOU LOOKING FOR IN THE HIVE?

What you need to look for in the hive varies according to the time of year and it will take experience to master. When you first start you seem to just stare, but within a few days of opening hives you will get plenty of practice at looking for things.

Finding the queen

The most important thing in the hive is a healthy queen, so you need to see her. This isn't always possible, but there are plenty of clues, such as eggs in cells. The queen lays an egg and during the first 24 hours it remains upright and takes 3 days to fall over prior to becoming a grub.

If you cannot see a queen you can surmise she is there by finding eggs, and the position of the egg indicates how long ago the queen was laying.

ESTABLISHING WHETHER THERE IS ROOM FOR EXPANSION

In the spring and early summer you need to know there is room for expansion within the colony, so make sure there are empty frames in the brood box, and if you cannot fit any more in – an unlikely event – consider having a second brood box.

The same applies to honey stores. Be sure there are always frames available for the bees to fill with honey. If they cannot store honey they cannot forage, and are likely to swarm.

Queen cells

Keep an eye out for queen cells. These are obvious: they look like peanuts hanging from the base of a frame or from the middle of a frame. They indicate the preparation of a colony to swarm. If you have a capped queen cell you may only have a day to do something about it, and we will go into this in greater detail later.

Brace comb and propolis

Bees will often build comb between the frames, called 'brace comb', and you can remove this. It isn't always necessary to do so as far as the bees are concerned, but it always makes it difficult to inspect the frames. I always take comb off the top bars of the frames too as, in another week, it would be really difficult to clear all the wax away without making a complete mess.

I harvest the propolis, which looks like a brown stain on the wood. Both wax and propolis are collected using the hive tool as a scraper. Wax is stored in a bucket for later use, propolis is scraped into a jam jar for dissolving in gin – an excellent gargle is created from this substance, but try not to swallow it.

FEEDING

At various times of the year you might wish to feed your bees. In the spring and summer add 1:1 syrup to a feeder that sits directly on top of the frames of the highest super.

You make this syrup by dissolving a kilo of sugar in a litre of water. It is always best to warm the water before you dissolve the sugar. Stir all the time and then allow the syrup to cool before use. In autumn you need 2:1 syrup, which is 2 kg of sugar to 1 litre of water. The difference is this second syrup is much closer to the concentration of honey, and the bees can usually store this by the end of September, if it is added in late August after honey is taken.

Winter feed is usually fondant. This is 4:1 syrup. (See recipe on page 126.)

HEFTING

The brood box plus a super of honey should be enough to keep your bees through the average winter. The only problem is there are very rarely average winters any more. Get used to feeling what your hive plus a super of honey feels like to lift. Then, whenever you are checking on the bees, heft again. If it feels lighter give the bees a feed of fondant as an emergency measure.

USING OTHER FEEDS AND APPLICATIONS

There are a number of feeds with nutrients of various sorts available for feeding bees instead of just sugar. They are not always necessary, but many beekeepers do swear by them. You will find all kinds of adverts for them in the beekeeping press.

Some hive treatments such as 'Hive Clean' are made from organic substances and are completely safe to use. In particular, 'Hive Clean' cause the bees to clean each other and significantly reduces varroa mite infestation, as well as making the hive a more disease-free space.

Bees use a great deal of water. They should have a way of collecting water that doesn't entail them drowning. I usually keep a tray of pebbles with some water in it so the bees can alight on the pebbles and drink.

SWARMING AND SUPERSEDURE

Bees reproduce themselves, and the way they do it is called swarming. It is intriguing to think it has something to do with the age of the queen, but in some years even a one-year-old queen will have her colony swarm. Bees know when it is important to swarm.

Swarming is nothing to do with absconding, when bees simply leave the hive in search of a better home.

Swarming starts with queen cells, and there are often more than one in a colony. The queen either lays an egg in the cells if the colony is reproducing, or in an emergency, an existing egg is chosen to become a queen. Previously, almost as a matter of course, the colony will have started to make drone cells in large numbers, often a prelude to the making of queen cells.

The queen cell is about 1.5 cm long and the young grub is fed royal jelly which is a fatty substance laden with proteins and enzymes that make the grub grow more quickly, and develop the ovaries.

The various queens develop and before release start to make a piping sound, a sort of scream whose purpose is not fully understood. Some say it is to warn other, still unhatched queens, they are coming to get them – personally I'm not so sure.

What is true is that the first hatched queen will try to kill the others, but is often prevented from doing so by the workers. A swarm might have a number of queens among their numbers.

Nuptial flights

Once she is ready, a virgin queen will fly, sometimes over a few days, among drones in order to mate. She will mate with a dozen or so males and then she has her fill of sperm, which she stores forever. It will take up to a month before the queen starts to lay her first eggs.

What can you do about swarms?

In the worst case, there is nothing you can do – if a colony wishes to swarm, it will, regardless of what you do to stop it.

First of all, give them room. The colony will swarm if there is not enough in the hive, so you can eliminate this causal agent by making sure they have enough space, both in the brood box and above. You can add another brood box, probably a super placed beneath the queen excluder. Such a set-up is called 'a one and a half brood'.

If your queen is new, you can kill all the other queen cells. Without a new queen there will be no swarm. But you have to be fastidious about it, and it is easy to miss them.

Artificial swarming

You can alternatively artificially swarm the bees, quite a simple technique, which involves another, empty hive or nucleus box. This is done in early summer.

Take three frames – four if you can manage it – of bees from your parent hive and put them in another hive at least 10 m away. Make sure there are eggs, grubs and capped brood in there. Shake the bees off another frame from the parent hive into the new hive.

Replace the frames with new ones, place a feeder on top and now you have two colonies. One with a queen, one without. Both colonies will think they have swarmed. If there are queen cells in the parent colony then either kill them, or kill your queen if she is old, along with all but one queen cell.

In the new colony, allow only one queen cell to develop. But if there are no queen cells in the new colony there soon will be.

All the flying bees in the new colony will return to their old hive. Within a month you will have two, fully functioning colonies. You must continue to feed the colonies with 2:1 syrup until they have grown in number to make them viable.

Shook swarm

This is a method of changing the frames in a colony that will also think it has swarmed in most cases. The importance of exchanging all the frames in these times of disease is important.

Move the existing hive a few metres away and build a new one in its place. Place the queen excluder *underneath* the brood box and fill with new, clean frames. Then remove the centre four frames.

In the old colony, find the queen and collect her in a queen cage or dry jar with a lid for safe keeping (make sure air can get in).

Carefully shake all the bees from the old colony into the hole left when you removed the frames. Replace the frames and then add the queen. Cover with a crown board and feed through the crown board hole with 2:1 syrup.

In a week the bees will have made up the cells and the queen will be laying happily.

How to collect a swarm

Bees that are swarming are great fun. For a start they are so full of honey and hormones they hardly sting – however, still make sure you are covered! Sometimes swarms can be lured by placing a hive or a box high up. Bees almost invariably climb when swarming. They are usually in a tree, or on a gutter or somewhere out of the way, so be careful, know how to use ladders and have someone to help.

Usually the swarm is simply cut off (as on a branch) and placed into a cardboard box, branch and all. The swarm can then be taken to their new hive.

At the hive, place a board from the entrance to the ground. On top of this place a white sheet. Be sure there are frames in the hive and a queen excluder if there is a super (not really needed at this point). Pour the bees onto the sheet and they will walk up the slope into their new home. Shake any bees that are stuck to the branch onto the sheet also. Feed the bees straight away, and within a week or so you will have a laying colony.

Swarm etiquette

You might think yourself lucky to find a swarm, but the truth is that some other beekeeper has lost one. Beekeepers are honour-bound at least to return swarms to their rightful owners should they become known.

MARKING A QUEEN

When you become experienced enough you can handle the queen easily, and dab her back with the appropriate colour for the year. However, you can use a tool, called a crown of thorns. It is a circular grille with spines all around. This is placed over the queen once found and gently manoeuvred so she cannot move. You can then mark her thorax through the grille.

COLLECTING HONEY

This is the goal of beekeeping, the reward. Straight away you are a thief – bees don't make honey for you, so make sure you leave them with some too. You can collect honey at any time, and if you move your bees around you can get several harvests of different types of honey in a season.

The main honey harvest is in the first fortnight of August, giving you time to treat for varroa and set the bees ready for winter by the end of September.

It is possible to remove the supers one by one, shake the bees off each frame and pop them somewhere out of the way, but this is a really cumbersome way of doing it.

Crown board

It is much easier to set a crown board underneath the super and one on top. Porter bee escapes will allow the bees to escape and not return (assuming you have them the right way round). The bee escape is an obvious piece of equipment to use and you slot them into the pre-drilled holes in the crown board.

It will take about a week for all the bees to exit the crown board and you can then (having checked for bees on the frames) remove the whole super.

It is at this stage you appreciate the beehive stand because a super full of honey weighs 15 kg, and you need to be careful about your back!

Remove the honey from the bees, preferably to a sealed box or room, otherwise they will only find it again.

Decapping

The honey is capped, so it will last, and you have to decap. This can be done either with a tool that looks like a steel comb, a decapping tool, or a hot knife. Use the frame as a cutting guide and try not to let the blade dig in too much. Save the cappings.

If you have one, a rotary spinner is a great way of getting all the honey out of the cells. This is basically a spin dryer with a special framework for the hive frames. Spin all your frames and then dispense the honey into jars with the special tap at the bottom.

Using a plastic box

For many years I used a food grade plastic box that allowed the honey to simply pour out of the decapped cells. It takes a lot longer, but it works. It is harder, however, to get the honey from here into the jars and if you want to sell your honey, you need 340g jars with labels.

You need a good tap to get the honey into the jars without making a mess of it and ruining your product.

Producing good honey

Local honey tastes so much better than the stuff you get in supermarkets that has been boiled and has a strong flavour. It should be clear, with no wax or air in it, and there should be no froth or ash at the top of the jar. You can filter your honey if you need to – I have found that honey judges in shows always know when you have filtered it!

RETURNING THE FRAMES

When you have finished your harvesting, put the frames back for a few days on top of the brood box, and the bees will lick out the residue and re-store it. The cappings can be placed on a warming table (you can buy special beekeeping tables) where the residual honey is melted off the wax. This then is added to your stock.

Alternatively, the cappings can be put in muslin and soaked in water ready to have more honey added to them to make mead (probably the best way of dealing with it anyway!).

CHAPTER 22

BEE DISEASES

There is a difference between a disease and an infestation. Your bees might have a lot of varroa mites, an organism that is currently destroying colonies around the world, and have major problems because of it, but there might still be healthy bees in the hive, untouched by the mite. However, varroasis is now classified as a bee disease because, sooner or later, the colony as a whole will show symptoms specific to the infestation of varroa mites.

This infestation will exacerbate disease problems and will present symptoms of its own. You might have small hive beetle (thankfully, it isn't in the UK at the time of writing), and the results will have enormous significance to your colony, but the bees themselves – apart from the chewed up ones, and the mess and the damage to the frames and the loss of honey – will be relatively unharmed as individuals.

Diseases, however, affect the individual bees directly, making them sick, either as eggs and grubs or as adult bees.

There are thousands of diseases and infestations a honeybee colony can acquire, just like people. Their major protection against disease is wax – a hard, waxy exoskeleton keeps most problems at bay. But there are two major problems for adult bees: one concerns the gut where they take in nectar, which can sometimes contain viruses, bacteria and protists (a whole group of single-celled organisms); the other concerns their breathing tubes or spiracles, which lead directly to the organs and tissues inside the bee.

A fair amount of disease is harboured inside the hive. Eggs and grubs do not have the same protection as adult bees, and there are many 'brood' diseases. The two

151

most common are the foul broods known as American foul brood and European foul brood.

PROBLEMS WITH BEE GENETICS

Genetically speaking, bees are not particularly good at reacting to environmental change. Compared to bacteria, bees have a low turnover of genetic mutations, and consequently, for an animal with a very simple immune system, it doesn't keep up with the faster breeding pathogenic organisms out there.

For example, a bacterial agent in a colony will double in number every 20 minutes. The average colony replacement time is two years, and although a queen will mate with ten or so drones, each having gone through genetic changes in its genesis, this represents a very low turnaround of possible useful mutations. Consequently, disease organisms respond to our attempts of removing them by becoming immune.

Varroa is a case in point. We used to treat them with a substance, a pyrethroid insecticide, that controlled the mite numbers. In time, the mites became immune, and other methods were needed to control them.

As soon as one problem is solved, another quickly replaces it.

WHY BEES CONTRACT DISEASES

The importance of cleanliness

There are a number of elements to bee diseases. The beekeeper has a role to play in keeping his bees as healthy as he can. It really is important you are hygienic in your beekeeping. Don't leave bits of wax or comb around the hive when you have been working in the hive and don't spill honey all over the place either. This is especially important when you are shaking bees off the frames because if there is uncapped honey in the cells, it will splash everywhere.

The reason for cleanliness around the hive is to deter stealing by other bees. This is a dangerous source of transference of disease from one colony to another. Bees steal honey from each other on a regular basis, and if you have left a piece of honey-soaked comb at the hive entrance, it simply acts as a beacon to alert any other bees and insects and, indeed, mammals, that there are bees nearby.

Always have a bucket handy to save your 'offcuts'.

The second aspect of cleanliness is your hive tool. Working in one hive, where the invisible spores for some disease may be lurking, you can easily move contaminants to the next hive, consequently infecting your whole apiary with the disease.

When working, always disinfect your equipment between hives. If you are used to wearing gloves, cover these with neoprene ones that you can discard and replace between hives. Don't lean on or over the frames, and try not to handle individual or groups of bees too much.

You can disinfect your hive tool by washing it in a liquid made of 50 per cent washing soda, and 50 per cent detergent in warm water. Wash it thoroughly then dry it and change your neoprene gloves before you open the next hive.

Don't use disinfectants: the aroma sends the bees into attack mode. They are not good with strong smells.

VARROA

The varroa mite is probably the most significant problem honeybee colonies face today and has been around for a long time. Its evolution and behaviour match perfectly the honeybee life cycle, but only in the recent generation have we had significant problems with it. Beekeepers will do well to remember the likelihood that varroa has been around for many tens of thousands of years in probable balance with honeybee populations, and that the change in the way we keep bees is the most likely cause of current problems. That and transport, because we have managed to move bee colonies far around the world.

Make no mistake, varroasis is a consequence of human activity. That said, the varroa mite is a serious problem for beekeepers, and has to be dealt with, otherwise your bees will die.

The treatment of varroa mites has changed over the years. Mites have become immune to various treatments, but the use of chemicals that are poisonous not only to the mites but the bees themselves leaves an opportunity to mention differential treatment.

Why does oxalic acid poison bees and mites, but the bees survive?

This information is valuable not only about varroa treatment, but because it holds true for many treatments in the hive, and is related to mathematics.

Surface area to volume ratio

If I take a cube and cut it in half, the volume of each piece has halved, which is obvious because we now have two smaller pieces where we had one larger piece. But the surface area of the cuboids has not reduced proportionately, because we have an extra face (the cut face) that now makes the surface area in relation to the volume a little higher. Repeat the operation and the surface area is bigger again, and repeated divisions mean the smallest pieces have a comparatively large surface area in relation to their volume. This is why powders, like flour, explode so very rapidly.

Now, apply this principle to bees and varroa mites: bees have a comparatively smaller surface area, when you take into account the area of all the spiracles etc., than varroa mites do. The varroa mite gets a bigger dose of poison, more quickly than the bees, and consequently dies while the bee survives.

Be careful when you are treating your colonies, because, if you overdo it, you will kill your bees as well as your mites.

The varroa floor

This was one of the major changes to the hive that, when it became popular, was such a shock. We were all constantly told the hive had to be kept warm, but in fact, the bees do that by themselves. Colonies in the wild are sometimes open to the elements and consequently feel no antipathy to an open-mesh floor.

When the mites fall off the bees, either through death, or more likely by being brushed or cleaned off, they escape the hive through the floor. This then means, either way, they cannot get back in and re-infect the colony.

However, the open floor has a drawback in that the bees have a draught going through the hive, so the top needs to be blocked off.

The varroa floor has a tray at the bottom to collect the mites as they fall, allowing you to count them. There is a direct correlation between the time of the year and the number of mites in the hive. It is possible to estimate mite numbers and take action accordingly.

Calculating the number of mites

This can be done at any time of the year, but June is probably the best for the summer, and will do as an example for now. Put the tray into the varroa floor and over a period of five days, collect the mites that fall out of the hive. Then get an average daily mite fall by dividing the total by the number of days you collected them for. Multiply this number by 30 (to represent a month) to estimate the number of mites in the hive. A figure less than 1000 is manageable. Over 1500 requires urgent and immediate attention.

The figure of 30 is a rule of thumb for June only. The varroa mite numbers vary according to the numbers of bees in the hive, so you get more in the summer than in the winter.

Calculating mite-fall is not that easy when you get older – you need sharp eyes! If you miss a couple of mites the calculation can be affected to a noticeable degree, so it is all only a guide, and if you have 1001 mites in the hive it isn't an automatic indication your colony is going to collapse.

There are a number of calculators on the internet which give an accurate indication of varroa numbers.

It's probably just as important you understand there are mites there and that you treat regularly and appropriately. The times to treat are in the winter, during late spring, late summer/early autumn.

Thymol

Thymol is a natural substance made from the herb, thyme, which is poisonous to insects and mites. However, when the dosage is correct, the mites are killed and the bees remain unharmed.

This makes for a smelly hive, and will taint the honey, so you generally use it after the honey has been taken, in late August/early September. The later you use it the less effective it becomes.

Thymol is usually simply placed on the brood top bars and left for a couple of weeks to a month. Individual instructions will be found on the particular product you use. Be sure to wear good gloves as the bees do not like it and attack. I have been particularly badly stung while delivering this treatment.

Sometimes the treatment is in biscuit form, other times it comes on a foil tray. If I have a double brood (two brood boxes – or indeed a brood and a half) the treatment is put right in the middle of the boxes.

A crown board is a good idea in order to make sure the vapours are high in the hive. Sometimes I have replaced the varroa floor with a solid one to decrease ventilation in the hive for the period of the treatment.

If thymol is administered correctly, it will kill about 95 per cent of the mites in the hive, so if you had 1000 mites in the hive in August, you would be left with 50. This number could easily re-infect the hive, so further treatments are important.

Oxalic acid

Once the mites are inside capped brood, no chemical can get to them and consequently treatments need to last for more than one 22-day cycle of brood, or should take place when there is no brood in the hive, which is usually winter.

Using oxalic acid is a case in point where only the mites that are actually on bees are killed. Consequently, in mid-winter there is very little brood about, and treating the bees to a dousing of 5 ml 3.2 per cent oxalic acid solution per frame of bees, poured from a syringe, is adequate to kill 90 per cent of the mites on the bees.

I have mostly done this with sugar solution, 1 kg sugar in a litre of water, with 75g of oxalic acid added. But you can get this ready made up.

Oxalic acid is a poison to humans too – wear gloves and always discard any surplus after treatment as chemical reactions in the bottle render it unsafe.

So, in the autumn and winter you have taken out about 95–99 per cent of the mites out of the hive, which is the major mite clearance time. However, this doesn't mean the treatments should stop during the summer.

Drone brood sacrifice

This is unpleasant for those of you who do not like to kill bees but it is quite effective. If the bees are allowed to make their own comb in the hive, they will produce a lot of drone brood, especially near Easter time. Put a super frame in the brood box and they will make it up. Once this brood is laid and capped, there will be a significant number of mites locked away in the brood and therefore you can take them away and destroy them.

This is a hard price for the colony, who made the wax, the grubs and fed them, therefore I try to do this only once a year.

Dusting with icing sugar

If you can cause the bees to clean each other, they will knock off mites in the process. A dusting of icing sugar can remove 15 per cent of the mites from the hive. Use a fine sieve to dust the sugar lightly so you are not causing an avalanche of sugar which will simply kill bees.

Natural oils and Hive Clean

There is a movement to use natural oils, wintergreen, patchouli, and others in the hive. These have not yet been tested properly. They may work but we don't know how effective they are. However, the product, Hive Clean which is simply poured over the bees in much the same way as oxalic acid (which it contains) is proven to be a very effective way of reducing mite numbers. You use it over a couple of brood cycles and you get high mite mortality. This product causes the mites to be cleaned off the bees and has a chemical action too. It can be used at any time of the year.

FOUL BROOD

This is a bacterial infection of the brood, one which smells and is rather unpleasant. The cells usually remain uncapped and the grub is found rotting away inside. It is a notifiable disease so you must inform your local bee inspector if you suspect you have it. The bee inspector will come and check your stock and, should he confirm it, your bees will be destroyed.

All your equipment will have to be disinfected and treated and you might decide to simply burn affected hives to make sure the bacteria is not lingering somewhere. Bleach is effective for plastic hives, a blow torch for wooden ones, and you must be scrupulously thorough.

There are two types of foul brood, American (AFB) or European (EFB), and in principle the results are the same for both.

The simplest test way to test for foul brood is to push a match stick into a cell, twist it a couple of times and slowly draw it out. The cell contents will hang off the matchstick like mucous from your nose when you have a bad cold.

THE SMALL HIVE BEETLE *(AETHINA TUMIDA)*

This beetle originated in Africa and has spread around the world because of the mass distribution of bees for commercial reasons. It was found in America in 1996 and has now spread to many states. Currently there is no small hive beetle in the UK, but there have been many scares. If we continue to import queens and bees from around the world it is only a matter of time before the beetle does appear in the UK, so be vigilant.

The beetles have most commonly been transported in hives. Commercial beekeepers in the USA have moved their bees in huge numbers to pollinate crops.

However, there have been reports of beetles being transported in boxes and packets – mostly during the purchase of queens.

The adult beetle is very heavily armed and is dark brown in colour. It looks a little like a vine weevil, only more robust. It is quite small, about 5 mm long.

Beetles lay eggs in the hive and the larvae, white in colour, eat pollen and honey. This activity causes the damage found in the hive. The adults live for half a year and lay many eggs, which become grubs that burrow through the frames, damaging and spoiling stores and frames.

In a hive there can be as many as 6000 beetles, which can be killed by pouring soapy water over them. The hive then needs to be torched or treated with bleach to kill any eggs. The woodwork must not be used for another year to be sure that no egg, secreted away in the nooks and crannies of the board, can get into the fray to start again.

The beetle pupates in soil, leaving emerging adults to reinfect hives. This can be avoided by drenching the soil around the hives. Although I obviously haven't had to do this myself, the drench is a strong soapy solution with something like Jeyes Fluid or bleach dissolved in it. If we ever do get this pest I imagine people will be moving their bees around to new sites very regularly.

Control
In the States a series of pesticides has been used, similar to those once used against varroa, in strip form. They are used on the floor, because this is where the beetles are mostly found. The strips are stuck to a piece of cardboard, and the beetles and larvae congregate beneath it and are killed by the vapours off the treatment.

NOSEMA
There are two forms of this disease, one in which the bees poo all over the hive and get sick and die, and the other when they just get sick and die without the pooing. *Nosema apis* is the dysentery form, *nosema ceranae* is the other. The latter form comes from the Far East and is treated in the same manner as the former.

The disease used to be called bee dysentery, which describes the pooing. The bees do get very sick. The agent is a single-celled organism which scientists have been unable to decide whether it is animal, fungal or something else.

The treatment remains the same, and is done by adding Fumidil B to the food, preferably in late August, so the bees that remain after the autumn decline receive a powerful dose.

Generally speaking, the colony doesn't do well, and it would be advisable to send a sample of your bees to your local bee inspector for analysis.

WAX MOTHS
In this country, bees can be affected by wax moth. This insect lays eggs in the hive, in a mass of webbing, and the grubs attack the comb. They can make a mess

inside the hive, but generally the bees are able to cope by themselves.

A good few days of freezing weather kills the moth, the grubs and the eggs.

If you have a problem you can use paradichlrorobenzene, which kills the insect.

CHALKBROOD

This is a fungal infection of larvae. The fungus appears mostly in wet conditions and will completely consume the larvae, leaving them white. The bees will clear out the mess, but the removal of the frame is a good idea. If you increase the ventilation in the hive you will usually deal with the problem.

Good feeding of the bees will also help.

STONE BROOD

The fungus that causes aspergillosis in mammals also devours larvae, turning them black and making them hard. The bees will clear out the dead bees and the colony will possibly recover, depending on how healthy it is. You can remove the frame if possible, and often, with good feeding the bees will do well.

Preparing a shook swarm, when bees are shaken into a new, clean hive, can also help.

TRACHEAL MITES

There are a number of mites that enter the spiracles of the adult bee and block them up. Isle of Wight disease is one such problem where the population of *apis mellifera mellifera* all but dies out in the UK.

You can see the bees struggling, holding their wings in a 'K' shape. Often the bees themselves can cope, but the use of both grease patties left on the frame tops and menthol are said to help. The Buckfast bee is said to be immune to this problem.

VIRAL INFECTIONS

There are so many viral infections that I don't intend to go into them, as they are off the radar for new beekeepers. However, Acute Paralysis Virus, Black Queen Virus, Kashmir Bee Virus and a dozen others are associated with (possibly) colony collapse disorder.

Fortunately, there is no colony collapse disorder in the UK. It might be tempting to blame this if your bees have starved, or succumbed to nosema without treatment.

SACBROOD

This is a disease caused by a virus you might well encounter. The larvae die at around the capping stage and are therefore found in capped cells. The body of the larva turns black, and if removed seems to be full of liquid.

It rarely causes a problem, disappearing when the bees are able to forage. The adults are not affected at all, and they remove larvae when detected.

Like all viruses, there is not much treatment, but it is a lesson to us all to keep our cleanliness up to scratch.

CHILLED BROOD

This is your fault. Opening the hive and exposing the larvae to cold temperatures will kill them. Adult bees are capable of withstanding quite cold temperatures, but larvae are not. Only expose larvae when the temperature is at least 15°C and always keep the exposure to a minimum. Workers will collect over brood in order to keep them warm, so be careful and patient.

INDEX

General
Brambell Report, 14

Cobbett, William, 2
composting, 8, 15
Cottage Economy, 2

Farm Animal Welfare Council, 13
Five Freedoms, 13

Hargreaves, Jack, 79

knowledge, 8

money, 3

philosophy, 4
Picture post, 79
plan, 8
runner beans, 9

Hens
Apple Cider Vinegar (ACV), 36, 65, 74

British Hen Welfare Trust, 57
breeds, 59–64
    Ancona, 61
    Australorp, 61

Bantams, 64
Barnevelder, 61
Black Rock, 62
hybrid, 60
Orpington, 62
Plymouth Rock, 61, 63
Rhode Island Red, 61, 63
Sussex, 63
Wyandottes, 63
broody, 17, 48, 72
bullying, 20, 66
buying, 57

calcium, 32, 37, 71
carry boxes, 31
chickens *see* hens
chicks, 72
cleaning, 53–5
clipping wings, 21, 71
cockerels, 18, 33, 52, 56, 73
combs, 65, 68

diarrhoea, 68
digestive system, 69

eggs, 16, 70
ex-battery hens, 52, 57

feathers, 15, 71
  missing, 67
feeding, 22, 32–9
fighting, 20, 52
fun, 16

garlic, 66
gravity feeder, 35
gravity water, 36

handling, 27–31, 73
hens, 8, 13–76
housing, 8, 19, 40–52
  building your own, 49–51
  introducing hens to, 51
  siting, 18, 20, 47
hutch *see* housing

immunisation, 22, 57

killing, 25

lice, 67
litter, 45

meat, 15
moult, 71

needs, 17
nesting boxes, 43, 51, 55

parasites, 18, 19, 22
perches, 44
permission, 3, 23–4
POL (point of lay), 59
poo, 16

Poultry Club of Great Britain, 16, 26
poultry parks, 58
problems, 66–8
protein, 32, 33

Raising Hens and Rabbits on Kitchen
  Scraps, 32
rats, 34
red mite, 19, 41, 45, 55, 68
run, 8, 19, 46–7

scaly legs, 67
sickness, 22
sunstroke, 21, 76

temperature, 21

ventilation, 42
vets, 22

wheezing, 68
worming, 37

Ducks
aspergillosis, 91, 106

bedding, 91, 104
breeds
  Aylesbury, 98–9
  Bantams, 102
  Call Ducks, 102
  Indian Runner, 93, 101–2
  Khaki Campbell, 92, 100
  Muscovy, 100–1
  Pekin, 99–100
  Rouen, 102

broody, 96
bumblefoot, 106
buying, 97

calcium, 86
cleaning, 91, 94
coccidiosis, 107

diseases, 104–8
drakes, 83, 98
ducks, 9, 78–108

eggs, 82, 91, 92–6
  breeds for, 92–3
  cooking with, 95
  removal of, 108
  storing, 95

feeding, 81, 84–7, 104
flies, 108
foraging, 82, 86
foxes, 86, 88

grit, 87

handling, 83
housing, 80, 88–91
  siting, 89
hygiene, 106

killing, 82

meat, 82
mites, 91
moult, 96

nest box, 81, 90–1

oyster shell, 86

parasites, 80, 107, 108
pellets, 85
poo, 81–94

ramp, 81, 90
roosting, 90
run, 81, 91

slugs, 80
starter crumbs, 84

vet, 105
viral enteritis, 106

water, 9, 80, 85, 105
worming, 80, 105, 107

young ducks, 105

Bees
anatomy, 114–19

beekeeping associations/societies, 10, 112,
  120, 130, 134
bees, 10, 111–63
  castes, 131
blowtorch, 125
brood box, 128
buckets, 124, 125, 153
buying bees, 134–5

chalkbrood, 161

chilled brood, 162
clothing, 121
crown board, 129, 148
crown of thorns, 147

decapping, 149
diseases, 115, 151–63
disinfecting, 124, 153
drones, 119, 132, 134

expansion, 142
experience, 120

feeders, 125, 126
feeding, 125–6, 136, 143
fondant, 126, 136, 138
foul brood, 158

hives, 127–30
hive tool, 118, 123
honey, 118, 137, 138, 147
    collecting, 147–50

medicine, 126
mentor, 130
mouse guards, 128, 138

nosema, 160
nucleus, 135

propolis, 124, 133, 143

queen, 118, 128, 131, 135, 141
    cells, 116, 128, 142, 144
    excluder, 128, 129
    marking, 132, 147

royal jelly, 132, 133

sacbrood, 162
siting, 10
small hive beetle (aethina tumida), 159
smoker, 122–3
sting, 118, 121
stone brood, 161
sugar syrup, 125
supers, 129
swarming, 137, 144–7
    artificial, 145
    collecting, 146
    shook, 146

tracheal mites, 161
treatments
    drone brood sacrifice, 134, 158
    Fumidil B, 126, 138, 161
    Hive Clean, 144, 158
    icing sugar, 158
    oxalic acid, 138, 154, 157
    Thymol, 138, 156

varroa mites, 127, 134, 137, 138, 144, 153–8

wasps, 128
water, 144
wax, 124, 140, 143
wax moths, 162
worker bees, 133, 139

year, 136-8